COUNTY WEXFORD

IN THE RARE OUL' TIMES

COUNTY WEXFORD 1910-1924

NICHOLAS FURLONG
AND
JOHN HAYES

We are extremely grateful to the following generous contributors
without whom this publication would not have been possible

Hilary Murphy, Consultant Editor

Robert and Avril Harvey • Rev. Patrick Comerford • Celestine Rafferty • Jarlath Glynn • Gráinne Doran • Billy Colfer
Bernard Browne • A.C. Nolan • Fionnuala Hanrahan • Muriel McCarthy • Garda Síochána Archives, Dublin Castle
Irish Army Archives, Cathal • Brugha Barracks, Dublin • Co. Wexford Library Service • John Power
Patricia Kinsella (nee Sinnott) • Dr. Austin and Mary O'Sullivan (nee Anglim) • Richard Roche • Paud Doyle
Séamus O'Keeffe • Eileen Berry (nee Dillon) • Theresa Gleeson • Eithne Scallan • Tomás Hayes • Jimmy FitzGibbon
Bernard Radford • Jim Doyle • Jim Sutton • New Ross Harbour Boat Club • Nicholas Cowman • Dan Walsh
Thomas Graham • Commandant Patrick Brennan • Dean Leslie Forrest • Canon James B. Curtis • Risteárd Mulcahy
Canon Séamus S. de Vál • David Parle Furniture, Ltd. • Ibar Carty • Robert Lambert • Maura Lambert • Ernie Shepherd
Mary O'Brien • Christopher Doyle • Wexford Harbour Boat Club • James Parle • John Brendan Nolan • Tim Scallan
Echo Newspapers • People Newspapers • Gerry Forde, snr • Helen Ashdown • Eamon Doyle • Helen Skrine
Joseph Culleton • County Museum, Enniscorthy Castle • Tony Furlong • Michael Fitzpatrick • Ken Hemingway
Maggie Ann Cousins • Breda Kelly • Patrick Kinsella • Liam Lahiff • Martin McCullough • Evelyn Cullen
Gerard Gaynor • Michael Ryan • Desmond Corish • Roger Sinnott • Shane Sinnott • Brian Cleary • Patrick Wallace
Peter McDonald • Jimmy and Sylvia O'Connor • Imperial War Museum, London • Philomena and Mary Byrne
Myles Redmond, jnr. • Nick Rossiter • Vincent and Ann Staples • Eva Hendrick • William White • Adoration Convent
James McGrath • John Sherwood • Patrick J. Jordan • Paddy Browne • Tomás Williams, Mary Farndon • Pat Codd
Mairéad Furlong • Jack O'Leary • Ian Hearne • Alan Owens • Eugene Field • Tim Pat Coogan • Aoife Larkin-Breslin
The Irish Railway Record Society • Irene Elgee • Alice Mernagh • Christina Jordan

Bank of Ireland

Old Distillery Press wishes to acknowledge the generous support and encouragement given by Wexford County Council
and the Bank of Ireland towards the publication of this volume.

Photographs and Donors
Since 1996 photograph donations have been made to us for this work. We have endeavoured to
trace holders of copyright materials. In a number of instances we have been unable to contact the specific
photographer while some of our donors are deceased now. We request that those who can help
us in identification would write to the publishers.

Front cover photograph: British artillery at Slaney Place, Enniscorthy.

OLD
DISTILLERY
PRESS

Old Distillery Press, Rosslare Road, Wexford, Ireland.

Copyright © Nicholas Furlong and John Hayes 2005

ISBN 0 9512812 3 2

Printed by Westside Press, Dublin

LIST OF PHOTOGRAPHS

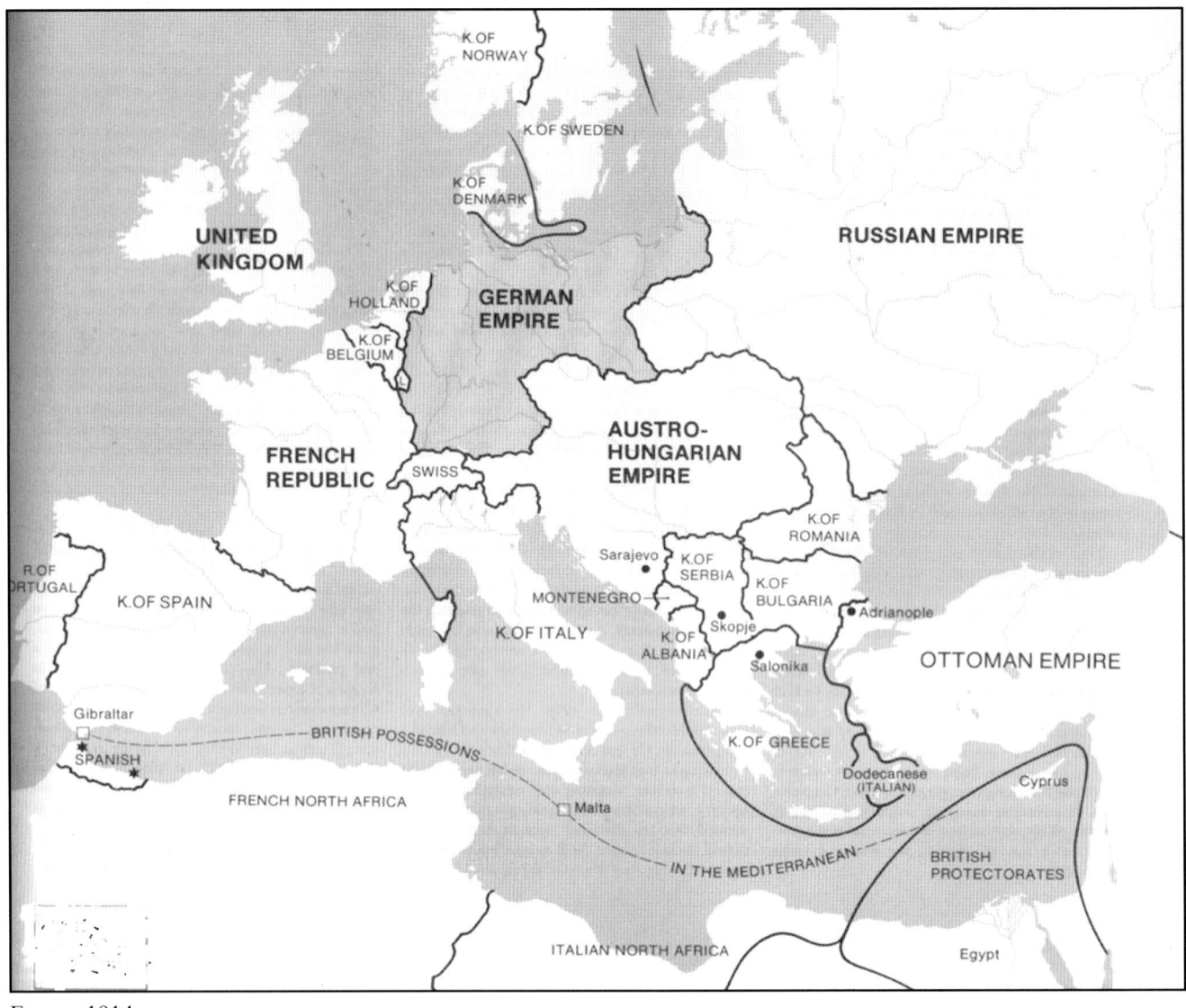

Europe 1914

County Wexford and War

The decade 1910 to 1920 was the most violent, the most horrific, the most catastrophic in world history to that time. When it was over many millions of young soldiers and sailors, the flower of Europe's youth, as well as civilians of all ages were dead.

The victors then created the conditions for an even more terrible world war. Millions of people were made to belong to countries they regarded as foreign in language and culture. Three new artificial states were created of which history had no precedent.

Czechs and Slovakians were stitched together and given angry minorities of Germans, Poles, Hungarians and Ukrainians to contend with. Yugoslavia was created with a mixture of Serbs, Croatians, Montenegrins, Macedonians, Slovenians and Albanians, three antagonistic religions – Roman Catholic, Russian Orthodox, Muslim and two separate, distinct written alphabets. In the island of Ireland a new statelet comprising six counties of Ulster's north east was created to facilitate a minority rigidly loyal to Britain and its monarch. The newly independent Poland received huge minorities of Germans, Ukranians and some Lithuanians

World War One erupted following the assassination of the heir to the thrones of the Austrian-Hungarian Empire, Archduke Franz Ferdinand, by a Serbian nationalist, Gavrilo Princip, on 28 July, 1914. It was a war between expanding imperial equals, rivals and colonists. With the possible exception of Romania and Serbia each power controlled, took possession of, administered and exploited vast areas of Africa, the Middle East and Asia. Even Belgium, proposed to Ireland's youth in propaganda as little, Catholic and mutilated, had vast possessions in Africa's mineral rich Congo. They administered their possessions with the extreme severity which Roger Casement exposed.

Were County Wexford an inland county its story in this period would have consisted simply of Ireland's persistent manoeuvres for independence from Britain, a major world power. The losses of Wexford people who answered John Redmond's appeal to assist Britain, since its parliament had "bestowed" Home Rule, would also be of unhappy record. Indeed had Ireland been geographically placed where Iceland is there would have been no reason for violence of any kind, national or international. However, since the early sixteenth century discovery of America's vast potential, Wexford and Ireland's geographic and strategic position placed her in a pivotal sea route position in every war between Europe's major naval powers.

Britain's accepted and determined possession of Ireland was neatly and unambiguously explained in Seavers biography of Archbishop John Gregg (Dublin 1963).

"It must not be forgotten that, besides internal discord and suspicions, external questions are involved. Many Irish political idealists would like to see Ireland as independent of Great Britain as Belgium is of France. And why not, say some. The war has given us the answer. Ireland's geographical position determines inevitably that it can never be a sovereign State. Ireland is the key to the Atlantic, and Great Britain, whose very life is bound up with the command of the sea, cannot allow the control of the coasts and harbours of Ireland to be in any but British hands. . . "

This innocent arrogance, akin to the French claims that Algeria was in fact part of France, reflects, however, the reality. The reality was the ruthless indifference of England's establishment to Ireland's claim of nationhood.

Submarine Warfare

In World War One, Wexford's position on the Atlantic approaches to Europe placed her directly in the area of a warfare never before experienced. It was submarine warfare on a grand scale which wreaked havoc off our Atlantic and Irish Sea coasts. This included the anti-submarine warfare using bases in Wexford by Britain and the United States.

In military terms the 1916 Rising in Dublin and Enniscorthy was lightly regarded by comparison with the murderous havoc of the battle zones in Russia, France, Belgium, the Atlantic and North Seas. Nevertheless, although the audacious gesture was repulsed in one week, the political and international effects were astonishing, profound and wide ranging. As Richard Mulcahy stated, "The aim of the 1916 leaders was to detonate the spirit of the Irish people." In this the events were to prove that the few succeeded spectacularly. It did not end with the detonation of Ireland's national spirit: it detonated the spirit of many peoples exploited, robbed and ruled, particularly as shown by Mahatma Gandhi in India.

It has been our aim in this work to rescue and publish for permanent record photographs taken during that period. It must be pointed out that due to the quality of many of the originals the finished reproductions would not be as we would wish but are published, nonetheless, because of their historic importance.

Comparatively few private photos of the War of Independence and particularly the Civil War have come to light. Despite the passing of eight decades families are still reticent about photographic reproduction. That reticence itself is evidence of a traumatic effect which lingers even to the present day.

We emphatically advise that the photographs in this volume do not represent adequate academic history. They are merely the photographs we have been able to collect from several family or other sources as well as those we have been allowed to reproduce. We earnestly hope that as a result more photographs in private collections or in seclusion may be made available.

Nicholas Furlong
John Hayes
August 14 2005

The new Europe reorganised by the victorious allies. The year is 1922.

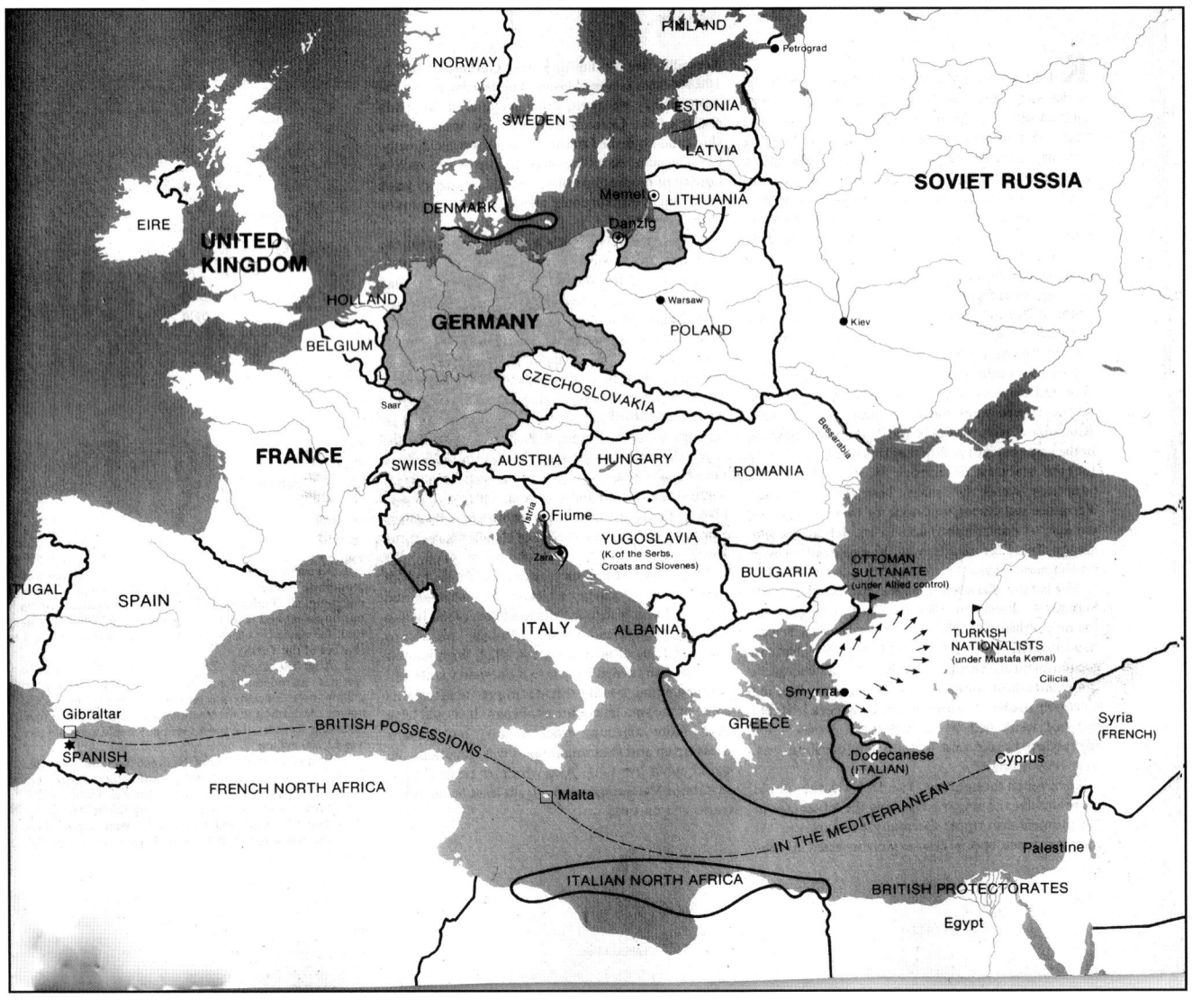

Our posed photograph of Duncannon Fort with its artillery pieces, ammunition, crews and fort children was taken in 1860, almost certainly by an official British Army photographer. In the face of military and naval technology with capital ships in later years, the fort's efficiency declined. These photographs, however, declare the continued strategic importance to England of the North Atlantic and the deep water entry into Southern Ireland which was Waterford Harbour. *(Duncannon Fort Maritime Museum Collection)*

RUMP OF EMPIRE

The Duncannon Fort garrison on parade in 1860. The British forces wore red coats and continued to do so for the next forty years. There are an estimated three hundred soldiers on parade. *(Duncannon Fort Maritime Museum Collection)*

Tents and soldiers on parade at Duncannon Fort 1860. Note the soldiers on the barracks rooftop. There must have been a reason for these poses even though the reason escapes us. *(Duncannon Fort Maritime Museum Collection)*

Posed photo of the actual gun crews. Two artillery pieces face out towards the sea. Seven cannons lie together, left of centre, with the shells. *(Duncannon Fort Maritime Musuem Collection)*

1901: Proclaiming the new reign of the King Emperor, Edward the Seventh, from the steps of the courthouse, Wexford. Listening on the court steps are newly elected nationalist Mayor, Benjamin Hughes, in robes and chain with uniformed mace-bearer; also councillors, officials, citizens, with the formal honour guard of the R.I.C. constables and sailors. The courthouse was blown up by the IRA during the War of Independence. Its comprehensive legal records were destroyed.

Recruiting for the Irish Guards 1901. Myles (Miley) Byrne, second from right, and father of Jack Byrne, Gorey, Irish Guards. The bounty for a recruiting sergeant in those days was worked on a sliding scale, five shillings for every recruit for the Brigade of Guards, no less than thirty shillings for one for the Household Cavalry. The Irish recruit was sent to the Guards' depot at Caterham home of the Brigade of Guards. The training and drill were difficult, to say the least, and their reward was nine pence per day. From this wage was deducted the cost of cleaning materials, haircuts, laundry and barrack damages. The cost of tobacco (1 oz.) or twenty cigarettes was three pence, and one and a half pennies for a pint of beer. The principal crime was drunkenness. *(Michael Fitzpatrick Collection)*

1912: New Ross Post Office staff, clerks, postmen and telegram boys. The only one we could positively identify before publication was the telegram boy at the left of our picture with the bicycle. He is Michael Hanlon.

Sheltered by the cliffs, the artillery battery at beach level in Rosslare is surrounded by its associated buildings in centre background. The original militia barracks, upland on the right, later became the coastguard station. We have been unable to obtain any closer photo. The base was built by the British Government to facilitate the training of the Royal Naval Volunteer Reserve. It is recorded that over 2,000 men did their annual training there and that the obsolete battle cruiser "Melampus" was attached to the base for gunnery, cruising and shore artillery practice. The installations had a 240-foot frontage with the sea. Rosslare in History (2005) states that the installations were demolished at the outbreak of the World War because the attention of the German high seas fleet was feared. The great guns were broken up and their remnants depressed into the beach. The massive foundations and three broken retrieved guns, two of them on the site, are all that remain to indicate the extent and function of the base.

A familiar colonial scene as Walker of Tykillen participation in an Indian hunting expedition is recorded. *(Tykillen Archives)*

The Emperor of Germany, Kaiser Wilhelm, with his cousin, King George of England, Emperor of India, in England. Each is wearing the uniform of the other as a gesture of friendship.

Polished carriage and immaculately clad and dressed pairs, with one odd passenger aloft, leave from the tidy famyard complex in Walkers of Tykillen. *(Tykillen Archives)*

Early Royal Irish Constabulary in Gorey. The pillbox hats were the first items of headgear worn by the Sir John Peel founded force. *(Michael FitzPatrick Collection)*

The early uniforms of the Royal Irish Constabulary members photographed at a rural north County Wexford Barracks, circa 1870, with their children.
(Michael FitzPatrick Collection)

Photos of the Carnesore lifeboat crew posed and taken in 1886. The emphasis is on the Cox, Paddy Kavanagh, who posed alone. He was one of the most famed and hardiest characters on the Wexford coast. Few lifeboats in the world were on so perilous a site as at Carnesore. Because of the vast number of ships lost where the Atlantic blasts into the Irish Sea up to the erection of Tuskar Rock Lighthouse, the place, the corner, was believed to be cursed. The ancients thought the Point of Carnesore to be possessed. That was the belief as far back as 190 A.D. when the map-maker of Egypt, Ptolemy, made his map of the known world from the accounts appointed sailors brought to him. He called Carnesore what the sailors called it in Greek, "Hieron Akron", or Sacred Promontory. This title has been interpreted as placation to the resident evil spirit by very apprehensive sailors.

WEXFORD'S TERRIBLE SEA

Carnesore lifeboat's famous coxswain, Paddy Kavanagh

Captain Eriksen (centre) and the surviving members of the crew of the "Mexico" on board the Wexford tug which helped in their rescue from the Keeraghs.
(John Doyle Collection, Fethard, by courtesy of Richard Roche).

THE WRECK OF THE MEXICO

On the twentieth of February in nineteen and
    fourteen,
The Norwegian schooner Mexico off the
    Wexford coast was seen,
From Lithuania to Liverpool with timber for
    the docks,
Now the gallant vessel lies a wreck on the
    savage Keeragh Rocks.

The Captain was a Mexican as you may
    understand;
The crew was made of strangers from many a
    foreign land.
Ten men in all their number, and hard was
    their fate I trow,
To take refuge in the island and leave the
    Mexico.

She was sighted first off Kilmore Quay and
    seemed in great distress;
The rolling waves and swelling seas did
    sorely on her press.
The Captain lost his bearings; 'twas the
    cause of bitter grief,
While Boreas blew with vengeance and drove
    them on the reef.

The lofty schooner was attired in double-
    reefed foresail,
Likewise she flew her mizen, but 'twas of no
    avail;
He tried to bring the ship about and head
    her off to sea,
But with the onslaught of the storm he could
    not get her stay.
The anxious crew worked hard then their
    precious lives to save,
Contending with the blinding sleet, and
    mountain-high each wave.
Two sailors in a small boat from her davits
    they let go;
They landed safe but failed to take us from
    the Mexico.

The Fethard men approached us then, in
    their life-boat strong and new,
To rescue us poor seamen who on the rocks
    were strewn.
Fourteen all told those hearts so bold, their
    courage was renowned;
But their boat was smashed upon the rocks
    and nine of them were drowned.

Thanks to our great Redeemer, the other five
    were saved,
And by their gallant efforts we were to the
    rocks conveyed.
We reached the Little Keeraghs by a halyard,
    as you know,
And bid adieu for ever to the ill-fated
    Mexico.

Our case was still appalling, as mountains
    rolled the seas;
Bereft of earthly succour for three long
    nights and days;
From the twentieth to the twenty-third, in
    sadness and in gloom,
We huddled on the island as in a living tomb.

The Wexford life-boat hove in sight and also
    the Dunmore,
But the Kilmore life-boat and her crew were
    driven back to shore.
Long life to Coxswain Wickham and his
    heroic life-boat crew;
He saved ten men from the jaws of death and
    the Dunmore life-boat, two.

There was deed of special daring, of courage
    brave and bold,
Performed by two of the Wexford crew; their
    names I will unfold:
Bill Duggan and Jim Wickham, in a small
    boat they did go,
And rescued the crew while the wild waves
    flew around the Mexico.

Here's a health to Captain Busher and his
    crew of gallant men;
To render their assistance with the Wexford
    tug they came;
Here's a health to every life-boat crew
    around green Erin's shore;
May God them steer from all rocks clear,
    now and for evermore.

These dangerous reefs, 'tis my belief,
    describe them best I can.
In their hidden treachery, they defy the eye of
    man;
They cause sad lamentations and tears in
    streams to flow,
As they did on the occasion of the ill-fated
    Mexico.

The ballad is taken from Fr. Joseph Ranson's
"Songs of the Wexford Coast", Enniscorthy
1948. The disaster inspired three separate
ballads. Our choice was composed by John
Codd, Blessington, Tagoat

After the storm the locals wait on Fethard beach as survivors of the "Mexico" disaster on the Keeragh island are brought ashore. *(Duncannon Fort Maritime Museum Collection)*

The Fethard lifeboat, the "Helen Blake", in 1914. The brave members of its crew were Patrick Roche, John McNamara, Christopher Bird, William Bird, Richard Bird, Garret Hendrick, Thomas Hendrick, William Banville, Patrick Cullen, James Morrissey, Patrick Butler, George Crampton, John Kelly and Michael Hendrick. *(Duncannon Fort Maritime Museum Collection)*

The surviving crew members of the Fethard Lifeboat "Helen Blake": Johnny McNamara, 2nd Cox; Garrett Hendrick, John Kelly, George Crampton and Richard Bird. *(Duncannon Fort Maritime Museum Collection)*

The widow of Patrick Cullen of the Fethard Lifeboat crew, who was drowned off the Keeraghs, with her nine children. She is the lady in black in the centre of the photograph with the infant in her arms. *(Duncannon Fort Maritime Museum Collection)*

Landing survivors of the
"Mexico"at Fethard Beach
in February 1914.
*(Duncannon Fort Maritime
Museum Collection)*

Bertie Downes landing mahogany logs at
Fethard Quay. They were from the wreck of
the "Mexico" and originally
intended for Liverpool. *(Duncannon Fort
Maritime Museum Collection)*

The crew of the Rosslare Fort lifeboat who took part in the "Mexico" rescue. They are from left, back row: John Walsh, Christopher Doyle, William Duggan and William Shiel. Front: Andrew Doyle, Philip Duggan, John Mitten, Mogue Furlong, Edward Wickham (cox), James Wickham (second cox) and William Walsh. *(Duncannon Fort Museum Collection)*

This photograph does more to highlight the "savagery" than a thousand words. It is the Mexico on the Keeragh Rocks. The ship is breaking up. This wreck and rescue operation was one of the most intensive on the Wexford Coast, certainly the most tragic in the era of photographs. The new Fethard Lifeboat was smashed in the rescue attempt and nine of the crew were drowned.
(Tomás Williams Collection)

Laying the foundation stone of the Bull Ring monument, Wexford, on Tuesday 1st November 1898. The old Tholsel, seat of the town's mayoral offices, with its arched alcoves to protect traders, is in the background.
(Tomás Williams Collection)

Annie Fenwick Jameson Marconi with her son and daughter. The former Annie Jameson of The Daphne, Enniscorthy, was the mother of Guglielmo Marconi, the inventor of the wireless telegraph which revolutionised communications. The world's first commercial use of wireless radio was made by him in Ireland in 1898 when wireless was used to report the progress of the Dun Laoghaire yacht races. Annie, a talented opera singer, was the daughter of Andrew Jameson who founded the famous Jameson whiskey distillery at Fairfield, Enniscorthy.

Contempt: "Misther Shpeaker, Sorr, wid the greatest re-spekt to yow, Sorr, I . . ." A London cartoon of an Irish MP at Westminster.

The hardy men of S. & A. G. Davis, Enniscorthy, with a white-collared office boy and an unmistakable gentleman of authority.

1914: James and Thomas Wickham reflect while seated upon a wall in the seemingly impregnable Fort of Rosslare. Holiday makers and their dog play on the nearby beach. Why should there be a need for concern?

HOME RULE FOR IRELAND

Home Rule for all Ireland, three times passed by the House of Commons in London, should have become law by the summer of 1914. It was violently resisted by the Ulster Unionists who formed the Ulster Volunteers in January 1913. They intended to oppose the meagre status of Home Rule for Ireland within the British Empire by armed force. Their slogan indicated their irrational fear: "Home Rule is Rome Rule".

The Irish Volunteers were founded in November 1913, with John Redmond as their chief. In March 1914 fifty-seven British Army officers at the Curragh declared their intention to resign their commissions rather than proceed against the Ulster Volunteers. In April 1914, the Ulster Volunteers imported a very large consignment of arms from Germany at Larne. The British Government then amended the Home Rule Bill to allow Ulster counties to opt out. At the end of July 1914 the Irish Volunteers landed their small consignment of arms from Germany at Howth. Ireland was on the verge of its own internal confrontation when World War erupted and the Redmonds chose the terrible gamble of supporting Britain in her time of danger.

John Redmond had to face a ghastly dilemma. The Ulster Unionist youth joined the British Army. If the Redmond Volunteers did not do the same in Britain's time of peril their dream of Home Rule being granted in friendship was in serious danger. The prevailing wisdom was that the war would be won by Christmas. The only thing to deflate that hope was the belief by the other combatants that they too would be home victorious by Christmas.

There had been a revival of Fenian republicanism since the 1798 commemorations. The sworn-to-secrecy Irish Republican Brotherhood, a legacy of the Fenian uprising, had been active. Irish Irelanders like Echo journalist Robert Brennan were numerous and influential. Frustration at Westminster's grudging gift of no more than county council status to Ireland became a festering sore. The Gaelic League and the GAA provided scope for more than just sports. Enthusiasm for the old culture in music, language and history claimed the young and not so young.

Promotion to join the British Army became intense and cunning. Posters and postcards were seductively designed. The Redmonds' oratory urged membership of the British Army nationwide. Their patriotic oratory of the 1798 commemorations was gone and replaced by new, amazing rhetoric. Disillusion crept in. The first casualty was John Redmond's Irish Volunteers who split into two antagonistic divisions. John Redmond's group was marginalised and regrouped as the National Volunteers.

In September 1914 the National Volunteers had 5,043 members in Wexford, the second-largest county membership in Leinster. Immediately after the split caused by John Redmond's support for the war, 438 joined the anti-Redmond Irish Volunteers. 715 Wexford men joined the British army in 1915 and 374 of these were Redmondite Volunteers.

John Redmond relaxing at home in Aughavanna.

Arthur Griffith, Dublin printer, founder of the self reliance movement Sinn Féin (We ourselves). He was given enormous financial support by a then anonymous County Wexford farmer – Pádraig Kehoe, poet, writer, patriot, of Enniscorthy.

Wexford's John Edward Redmond, M.P., leader of the Irish Nationalist Party in Westminster, addresses a Home Rule meeting in Dublin in 1912. He was one of the greatest orators of his day. He used the legal Westminster parliamentary system to win Home Rule for all Ireland, a meagre measure though violently opposed by British Unionists in Britain and Ireland.

William Redmond, M.P., at the height of the Irish Nationalist Party's prestige in Ireland and amongst the Irish world-wide, with admirers during his visit to Australia in early 1914.

Irish Volunteers on a cycling exercise at Rosslare Strand before the split of 1914. Kelly's Strand Hotel, and little else, form the background.
(Alice White Collection)

Anti-Home Rule meeting of Counties Wexford, Carlow and Kilkenny Unionists in Kilkenny Castle. *(Shane Sinnott Collection).*

WANT, HUNGER, BITTERNESS

The bitter industrial strife and lockouts in Wexford of 1911-12 is still a matter of sorry memory. Wexford was the centre of the agricultural machinery industry at a time when the horse economy was at its zenith. The tough implements hurtled forth across the world, packing Ireland first and then promoting the reputation of Wexford for reliability in a mighty world axis, which stretched from Argentina to Romania. This satisfactory situation, which should have benefited all, turned suddenly and ferociously sour in 1911 when the huge Wexford workforce demanded better pay and conditions, along with the right to form trade unions of their choice. The outcome is now history of so ferocious a memory that it was actually shunned in open conversation. The opportunity to turn the suffering of the workers and their families to beneficial potential was not lost and the memory still rings of the oratory of Big Jim Larkin, P. T. Daly, Dick Corish and James Connolly at the Redmond Monument and elsewhere. The massive foundry works with order books filled ground to a halt. Desperate, the employers brought in scab labour under armed guard. Our photograph shows the scab labour force being escorted to work in Pierces Foundry by R.I.C. constables in King Street, Wexford. *(Alice White Collection)*

Pierces Foundry office staff 1911. *(Alice White Collection).*

The last pay-day in Pierces. The workers women and family members wait outside the main gate on Distillery Road.
(Alice White Collection)

Very relaxed relief R.I.C. constables sent to Wexford during the 1911 lockout. In front, most relaxed: Constables Glennon and Campbell. Second row: O'Grady, Kelly, Carney, Lennane and Martin. Third row: McGosham, Moore, Edward M. Gordon, Johnston, Donovan, Byrne and Keenan. Back row: Hobbs, Kennedy, Quirke, Gleeson, McAtarsney. The two local boys were the Thomas brothers.

1912 in Wexford, as in Dublin, brought the first major commercial revolt in the century. In a curious way it mirror-imaged the manner in which the bloody 1793 clash between countrymen and militia at Wygram facilitated the 1798 Rebellion. The strike basically was for the betterment of pay and conditions prevailing amongst the large workforce in the agricultural machinery industry, which in Wexford consisted of three thriving factories with developed national and world-wide outlets. The bitter debates over the rights of workers and the rights of employers blighted the notion that they were partners in enterprise.

Richard Corish, Wexford's hero of the 1912 workers defiance, in later years at a Bullring rally. He retained his vigour and spell-binding oratory which rallied the workers of 1911 and 1912.
(Photo by courtesy of Desmond Corish)

Royal Irish Constabulary
reinforcements in George
Street Barracks, Wexford,
during the 1911 lockout.

1911-12 Lockout. R.I.C.
constables escorting raw
materials to Pierces
foundry from the quayside
or North Railway Station.
(Alice White Collection)

1911-12: Machines for export escorted along Wexford Quay by the R.I.C. from Pierces Foundry. *(Alice White Collection)*

National Executive, Irish Trade Union Congress and Labour Party, 1914. Standing: James Connolly, William O'Brien, M. J. Egan, Thomas Cassidy, W. E. Hill and Richard O'Carroll. Sitting: Thomas MacPartlin, D. R. Campbell, P. T. Daly, James Larkin and M. J. O'Lehane, James Larkin, James Connolly, later executed after the 1916 Rising, and P. T. Daly came to Wexford to give massive support to the striking and locked out workers in the 1911 confrontation. Connolly and Larkin stayed with the dynamic Wexford workers' leader, Richard Corish, in his home at 35, William Street. Larkin, P. T. Daly and Dick Corish were accused of "inflaming class hatred" but P. T. Daly, a member of the Irish Republican Brotherhood, was vigorously pursued by the partisan establishment. In January 1912 he was sentenced to three months in Waterford Jail for incitement. The Sinn Féin activist, Seán Etchingham of Ballynatray, Courtown Harbour, succeeded in having the proceeds of the Leinster senior hurling final, between Dublin and Kilkenny in Croke Park, donated to the Lockout Fund. Hard concessions were won and work was resumed on 12 February 1912. *(Larkin Family Collection)*

Matthew J. Furlong at his premises in South Main Street, Wexford. A defiant patriot all his life, he was a founder member of the Gaelic League inspired by Dr. Douglas Hyde, a founder member of Sinn Féin in County Wexford and a brilliant business publicist. His large advertisements in the Wexford papers in the early years of the twentieth century were creations of sheer and delightful genius.

Gaelic League and Irish Ireland revival shown in Wexford, undoubtedly for a Feis Ceoil or a Gaelic League concert. At left the inspirational but ill-fated Liam Mellows. The elderly lady is Mrs Ellen Sinnott, nee Brady of Cavan, mother of the War of Independence veteran John Sinnott of Grattan Terrace, Wexford. To her left is Mrs Larry Duggan of School Street and standing at right is her sister Mrs Moira Larkin of Grattan Terrace. Both girls became active War of Independence members of Inghíní na hÉireann.

(Seán Sinnott family Collection)

"These men are prepared to die for their convictions . . ." Ulster Volunteers in training, 1914. *(Shane Sinnott Collection)*

Ulster Day 1912. Anti-Home Rule leaders, including Carson and F. E. Smith, marching to the City Hall, Belfast, for the signing of the Ulster Covenant. *(Shane Sinnott Collection)*.

THE FIRST WORLD WAR

On 28 June 1914, Archduke Franz Ferdinand, the heir to the Austro-Hungarian throne, was, along with his wife, assassinated in Sarajevo by a Serbian nationalist. Within five weeks this single event had triggered a war involving every major European imperialist nation with the exception of Spain. The British government authorised the raising of six new army divisions. One of them, the 10th Irish, began forming followed by the 36th Ulster formed from the U.V.F. The youth of the belligerent nations joined their colours with enthusiasm, as if it were going to be a short term adventure.

Our boys on the way to the front. "Come and join us", they seem to say in this homeward bound postcard. It is a studio photo, one of thousands sent back, but it has the message of military comfort. There's a tent at the right, while the soldiers, spick and span, hold cigarettes and have no care. On the left is Charlie Valentine, a Gorey painter and champion runner. His family were caretakers of Gorey Courthouse.
(Michael Fitzpatrick Collection)

Propaganda Poster. "The real Irish spirit," complete with shamrocks, Lake of Killarney, round tower and ruined abbey. This prompted, it was hoped, the impeccably clad Irish buachaill to exchange his robes for that of a British army soldier on the Western front's trenches.

Group of Enniscorthy Irish Volunteers pictured before the divisions of 1914. Presented by Mrs. T. J. O'Neill, John Street, Enniscorthy, daughter of Walter Sutton who is included in the photograph (second row, third from left). The spirit of Vinegar Hill is clearly invoked in the photograph. The Irish Volunteers were formed on November 25th 1913. The split was initiated on September 24th 1914, when, following John Redmond's vigorous support for the British war effort, his leadership of the Volunteers was repudiated. John Redmond's supporters in the Irish Volunteers reformed and renamed as the National Volunteers.

New boy recruits from Adamstown for war and adventure on the Western Front.

Plenty of time for fun and recreation as this postcard home to Wexford from somewhere on the Western Front shows! "I cannot write where we are but Jack and me have plenty time for boxing." *(Anonymous donor)*

Wexford District members of John Redmond's National Volunteers. The flag at left was the old Irish flag, gold harp on greeen. The flag at right was another old Gaelic flag with the sunburst and beams motif. Seated: Patrick Clampet, P. Donovan, Mr. Wilson, Patrick O'Connor and James Breen. Standing: Joseph Scallan, J. Wall, John Doyle, Thomas Barnes, and, at extreme right, J. Donovan.

Photographed in or about 1916 is a typical Wexford British officer class family. It was taken at The Raven, Curracloe, when three of the remarkably alike O'Toole brothers were home on leave. Standing: Jack O'Toole, Kathleen Thomson, Pennie Lewis, Larry O'Toole, Peig and Jack Elgee (solicitors, George St., Wexford) Ella Thomson and Ned O'Toole. Seated: Polly O'Toole, grandmother and grandfather O'Toole, Nancy and Hennie O'Toole. The children are Editha Roark, Edward Lewis and Robert Roark. *(Irene Elgee Collection)*

(Tykillen Archives)

World War One communications at the front required the use of carrier pigeons. Whether the one in the photo is a parrot or pigeon is open to debate but the photo of a Walker of Tykillen taken in France is authentic. *(Tykillen Archives)*

John Redmond addressing Irish Volunteers weeks before the movement split. *(Echo Newspapers)*

POSTCARDS FROM THE FRONT

Capt. Frank Staples.

One of the most faithful communicators from the Western Front to relations in County Wexford was Captain Frank Staples, MRCVS of Rathjarney. He was a popular skilled practitioner and colourful character in his South Wexford veterinary practice for the greater part of the twentieth century. While operating, injecting or castrating, he never stinted his listeners with views on politics, war experiences or denunciations of the unhygienic. Those experiences, education and contacts made him brimful of startling and wide areas of information. For example, he was a fellow student in Blackrock College of Eamon de Valera, Professor Alfred O'Rahilly and the later Cardinal John Dalton, Archbishop of Armagh, Primate of All-Ireland.

As most people in County Wexford were, early in the decade, Frank Staples was an admirer of John Edward Redmond and responded to his call to enlist in Britain's hour of certain peril. From 1914 he sent back postcards regularly, sometimes four or five at a time, showing scenes of war and devastation with an emphasis on damaged churches in France which undoubtedly raised the required ire. Early in the war he could say where exactly he was on the cards. Later the censor saw to it that no such information was posted on. Nevertheless he did manage to pass on comments which were most interesting in the light of subsequent events.

Naturally he served with the Royal Veterinary Corps and at one stage while on the Aisne River was subjected to an exceptional heavy German bombardment. Such was the devastation that he was the only ranking officer alive in his sector, but certainly of no military authority or experience.

The town of Arras devasted by German bombers in 1914.

The town of Arras seen after the bombing by the Allies in 1914

German troops on a supply mission in 1914

An Irish sergeant with twelve surviving men approached him and said, "Begor, sir, I think we'd better be getting out of here," to which Captain Staples responded in the vernacular, without incrimination, "Begor, sergeant, I think that would be a good idea." And so he lived to tell the tale.

The quotations are from his postcards which are mostly headed OAS (On Active Service). On this first card, Bray-sur-Somme has been pencilled out by the censor. " . . . .*the traffic on this road for the last fortnight is tremendous. However when you see the other poor chaps it is no use grousing. We are very well off. (This P.C. of a farm near the old place must have been taken before the war days as the Huns used to shell it very often). I sent 3 photos to George of myself and a friend from the "Black North". I suppose you have got one of them by this. I have one squadron of N.I. Horse under me this last week. They are practically all north men. I don't know any of them."*

31-5-16 *"Just a little to the right of the trees* (on the postcard) *the most of the Boche shells dropped when they shelled us last Saturday week morning at the back of the trees in the churchyard - F.R.S."*

By the latter part of May 1916 news of the Rebellion in Dublin and Enniscorthy reached the front line, probably with little detail so its extent or aftermath may only have been guessed at. This to his sister, "Sis" in Scar Castle, Duncormick. *". . . I will get leave before that time. I am sure you had an exciting time during the Rebellion, you have such a large no. of S.F. around you. Well I think they did a lot of harm to the old country. Baby* (another sister) *had told me about the*

labour trouble but I suppose at the way things are you are very lucky to get labourers at six shilling per week. I think if they only knew the wages that are here . . ."

To his sister, Baby Staples, Rathjarney. 14-10-17.

"So far we have not definitely heard where we are going to. However we have a fairly good idea of where it will be and I daresay you can guess. We hear pretty bad stories of it but hope it won't be as bad as it is painted. We are having very bad weather."

(Somme region, undated) *". . . The country round is greatly changed since new roads, new railways and everything else pertaining to war. Burial grounds galore and new inhabitants for them every day. I saw some Irish names in them but no one I knew, mostly Irishmen in English regiments. I have been in some of the captured villages and what was left of them. Everything in ruins, also the trenches. The German trenches simply knocked to pieces and the ground just behind them every yard of it I might say ploughed."*

To his sister Mother Evangeline, Loreto Convent, Dalkey (from the Somme area, a village taken by the Germans and retaken by the British) *"I rode in on two occasions (a half horse ride), it is the same old place and was*

A French cycling corps moves up near Ypres in Belgium

Cambrai in winter following German bombardment

not harmed. I am on the other side of it this time. The country has undergone great changes since, new railways, new roads and troops, troops, troops. Burial grounds all over the place and of course new inhabitants every day."

July 1 (1917?) *". . . At Gommencourt. On leaving Warlincourt we marched to Doullens, stayed there for night, next day went on to Fruhen-le-Grand. Stayed there for a night. Next day marched to St. Riquier. We stayed there until 3 Sept. Left that day."*

We are grateful to Mrs. Eva Hendrick, nee Staples, Rathjarney for allowing us to examine and reproduce samples from the family's valuable collection.

French troops in retaken Carency with captured German artillery, 12 May 1915

A lone British "Tommy" in Captain Frank Staples zone of operations.

John Edward Redmond, M.P., leader of the Nationalist Party in Westminster, was an inspirational speaker from the Land League, Parnell and 1798 centenary days. His mastery and voice volume would have never required a microphone. This press photo from the London Daily Mail carried a caption "Redmond Rallying Irish Volunteers to the Flag" with further words which had they but known or cared, only nourished cynicism. It states "Recalling the brilliant exploits of Irish soldiers on the Continent in days past, Mr. John Redmond declared at a great gathering of Nationalist Volunteers, 'The manhood of Ireland will insist on maintaining bright and untarnished on the battlefields of Europe the reputation of our soldiery.' Irish recruits are rushing to the colours," the Daily Mail added. There is not a uniformed Volunteer in sight. It is an election meeting in Wexford's Bullring.

In order that there be no confusion, the group of Gorey Irish Volunteers proclaim their identity following the split from John Redmonnd's National Volunteers. Joe Stafford, Patsy Dwyer, Bill Tomkins, Peter Connolly, Aidan McLeod and Thomas Dugdale.
(Michael Fitzpatrick Collection)

Dinnie Byrne, Gorey's Town Crier, 1915

Shell cases ready for
delivery from Pierces
(Alice Whie Collection)

Munition cases for despatch from Pierces by
rail. A British soldier stands in the
background. *(Alice White Collection)*

PIERCES

MANUFACTURE

SHELL CASES

Munitions for the British army were manufactured in Wexford. Pierce's farm machinery factory made shell cases in huge numbers.

As the war dragged on casualties mounted to an appalling degree. County Wexford's newspapers were weekly reporting deaths, in the mud of he Western Front. In the early days of the conflict the obituaries had a note of shock or of improvided loss. By the end of hostilities even the civil words of comfort had been debased. Britain facing imminent defeat intended to extend conscription to Ireland. This threat had the effect of rousing the county and country in oppositon. The church as well as the population were so determined on this issue that conscription was never imposed.

Shells for the British Army being manufactured in Pierces. *(Alice White Collection)*

Shell cases in assembly
line manufacture in
Pierces.
  (Alice White Collection).

THE 1916 RISING IN ENNISCORTHY

The national spirit in Wexford had grown but it was with a sense of pride in Ireland and of Ireland that it prospered. There were rapid nationalist strides since the first years of the decade in Wexford town, New Ross, Gorey and Enniscorthy. There was another political party and concept. It was the political movement founded by a Dublin printer, Arthur Griffith. It was given the Irish name 'Sinn Féin'–We Ourselves.

Adherents came from all parts of Co. Wexford and the movement was well consolidated by 1915. Inevitably, bitterness arose between those who supported Britain in the war and those whose focus was on complete independence for all Ireland. The Irish Republican Brotherhood worked in secret. New volunteers to this radically nationalist organisation were sworn in by a senior Dublin member, Sean T. O'Kelly, in John Barker's premises in South Main Street, Wexford. On 26 September 1915, the Wexford Brigade of the Irish Volunteers was sufficiently ready to be reviewed and addressed by Commandant Patrick Pearse on Vinegar Hill. Cumann na mBan had been organised to facilitate the contributions of women.

Military manoeuvres were ordered for Easter Sunday, 23 April 1916. Eoin MacNeill, chairman of the Volunteer Executive and Chief of Staff, favoured defensive action only. Other executive members determined there should be a rising before the war ended, "if only to redeem the national honour", Robert Brennan recalled. Enniscorthy was to be taken over by the Volunteers, but on Sunday the 'manoeuvres' were called off by Eoin MacNeill. However, news that the Dublin Volunteers had risen and occupied the city's major buildings was confirmed. That was sufficient for the Wexford leadership. Enniscorthy was taken over, with the Athenaeum Theatre used as a headquarters. It may be that the Volunteers did not realise that, with the exception of Dublin and a couple of small centres, MacNeill's countermand had been obeyed.

From a military point of view the rebels were in an untenable position. Artillery could dislodge them and level the town. There was, however, a deterrent to that solution. The rebels controlled the railway tunnel through which British Army reinforcements would travel towards Dublin from Rosslare. Caution was preferred. In the event the British Army commander in the county was himself a Wexford man, Colonel French of Newbay.

Despite the surrender of the Dublin Volunteers at the end of Easter week, Enniscorthy's leaders refused the demand to surrender. They would only surrender if ordered to do so by Patrick Pearse. This order was obtained and Co. Wexford's part in this phase of rebellion was over. 270 were arrested, of whom 150 were interned at Frongoch in north Wales. Nine County Wexford men were courtmartialled and six sentenced to death, but their sentences were commuted. Dublin-based Michael Hanrahan of New Ross was executed.

Irish Volunteers in Enniscorthy

There are many photos of 1916 in Enniscorthy. This photo includes a party of Irish Volunteers from Wexford town and Ferns, men who were prominent in the national movement. It includes one of the best known senior officers in the county in 1915-1916 and subsequently, teacher Myles Redmond, seated in his hair in the left foreground. He is mentioned frequently in Robert Brennan's memoirs, "Allegience". It was taken at the 1798 statue in Enniscorthy's Market Square on September 29th 1915. This took place at a gathering of all the county's Irish Volunteers addressed by Pádraig Pearse.

We are grateful to the Byrne sisters of Patrick Square, Wexford for this record. The photo has some fire damage. Kneeling with rifle between the two men with Irish Volunteer ranger hats is gent's hairdresser and band musician, Tom O'Byrne of Patrick Square, Wexford. His brother, Pierce, is alongside him on his left with raised rifle. The man in the back row at centre with the soft hat, heavy moustache, shouldered rifle and bandolier is Laurence Cummins of Waterloo Road, Wexford and Ballymurn.

'98 Pike

The pike-bearing Volunteer at the back at the memorial is Thomas Roche of Ferns. The Volunteer directly in front of him is Edward Foley of Crossabeg and North Main Street, Wexford. Fourth from right in the back row is James Cullen and to his left is Patrick Keegan. There's a set of bagpipes in the foreground. This is the only photo of the period that we have seen with a pike carried as a weapon. In the shortage of guns and ammunition hundreds of pikes were forged in Co. Wexford prior to 1916.

A party of Irish Volunteers from Enniscorthy, Ferns and Wexford.

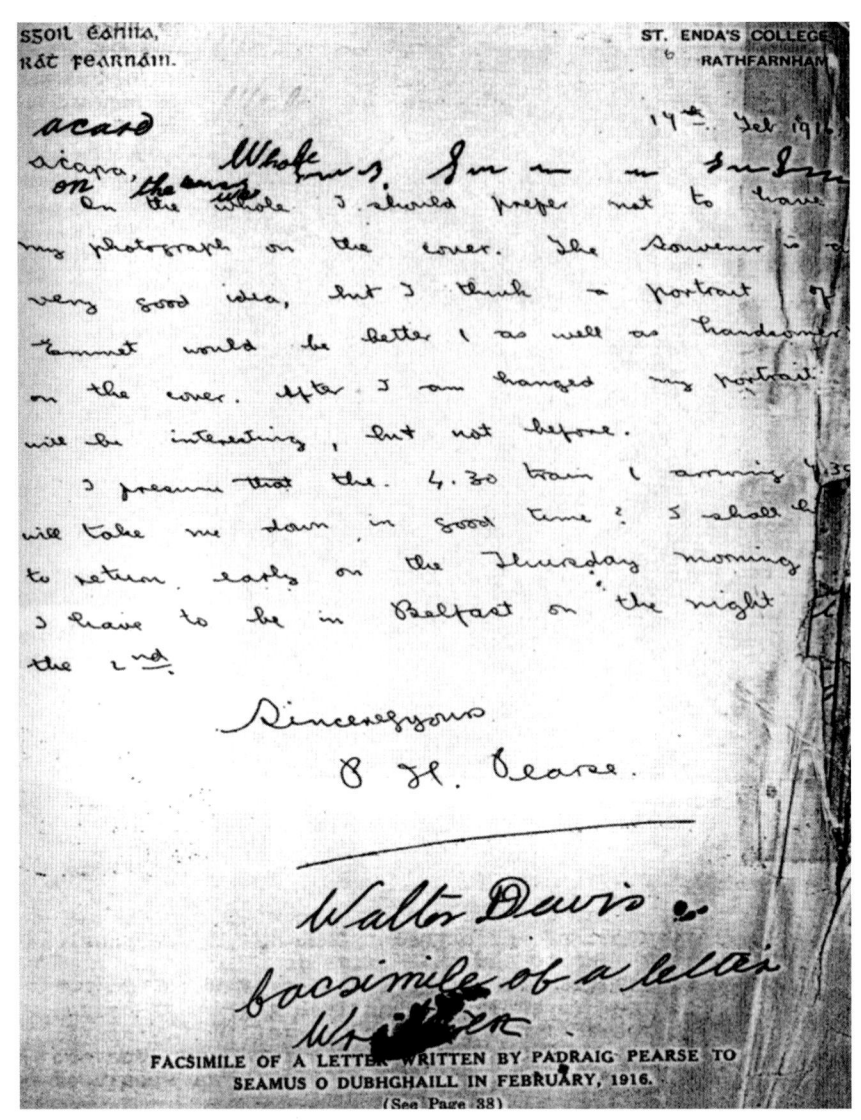

FACSIMILE OF A LETTER WRITTEN BY PÁDRAIG PEARSE TO
SEAMUS O DUBHGHAILL IN FEBRUARY, 1916.
(See Page 38)

Historic letter written by Pádraig Pearse in February 1916. It will be remembered that Pearse came to Enniscorthy on 1 March 1916 to deliver an oration at the Emmet Commemoration Concert. Seamus Doyle wrote to Pearse asking him for a portrait of himself to put on the cover of the Concert Programme. This letter is Pearse's reply. Written on Sgoil Éanna notepaper. It reads:
'A Chara,
'On the whole I should prefer not to have my photograph on the cover. The souvenir is a very good idea, but I think a portrait of Emmet would be better (as well as handsomer) on the cover. After I am hanged my portrait will be interesting, but not before. I presume that the 4.30 train (arriving 7.39) will take me down in good time? I shall have to return early on Thursday morning, as I have to be in Belfast on the night of the 2nd.'
(Courtesy of Mrs Mary Farndon, Blackstoops, Enniscorthy)

I rish Volunteers in Enniscorthy before the 1916 outbreak. Back row, left to right: Johnny Connolly, Felix Murphy (Blacksmith), Ed. Ryan, Ed. Murphy (Springvalley), Pat Adams, Dinny Kehoe, John Ryan, Watt Sutton, Jack Hughes, Ml. Pierce, Jess Murphy, Stephen O'Connor, Tommy Waters, Robt. Goff, Paddy Wildes, Patk. Murphy, Tom Boyne, Jas. Roche (cotman), Tom Jordan, Mike Askins.

Second row: Jos. Franklin, J. Dwyer, Robt. Corrigan, Con Franklin, Matt Leacy, Bob Hawkins, Paddy Johnson, Denny Dwyer, Myles Roche, Andy (Lar) Doyle, Patrick Webster, Ed. O'Connor, Martin Kehoe, John Kenny, Ml. O'Toole, Martin Kehoe, Lce. O'Neill.

Third row: Jack Balfe, Jas Martin, Ml. Balfe, Tobias Murphy, Jas. O'Neill, Syl. Balfe, Patrick Corrigan, (-), Mike O'Connor, John Purcell, Wm. Quirke, Paddy Pierce, Patrick Hall, William Sheehan, Ml. Sheehan, Aidan Kenny, Jos. Callaghan, Andy Kehoe, Ml. Doyle,. Har Habbernatty, Patsy O'Farrell.

Fourth row: Robt. O'Neill, A. Mullett, Patk. Boyne, Jas Deegan, John Forrestal, Ml. Murphy, Bob O'Connor, Robt. Webster, Jack Leacy, J. Tobin, Clem Kelly, John Wafer, Mikey Murphy, John Boyne, Jimmy Murphy, 'Kerr' J. Whelan, J. Murphy.

Fifth row: John Murphy, Robt. O'Neill, Jim Ryan, J.J. Cosgrave, Alec Doyle, Ml. Cahill, John Parker (Dave and Wm. O'Reilly, Boy Scouts), John O'Reilly, Art and Patk. Carton, Patrick Dempsey, Jas. O'Neill, Tom O'Neill, Ed. McDonald, P. Dempsey, Owen Leacy.

Sixth row: John O'Leary, Felix Murphy, Jas. Ringwood, Tom Toole, Owen Hiney, Wm. Hiney, John Carley, Paddy Doyle.

Scouts: Martin Doyle, Pat Kehoe, Paddy (Red) Boyne, Ml. Cowman, Chris O'Toole, Tom Kehoe, Jas. Goff, John Cullen, Paddy (Black) Boyne, Ed. Woods, Peter Murphy, Harry Goff, Syl Blafe, Tom Murphy, Jim Quirke, Patk. Woods, E. Goff, Tom Brooks, Geo. and Wm. Meyler.

Bandsmen: Tom Bishop, Edward Ryan and Martin Leary.

Photo taken in Bennett's ball alley by Alfred Creane, Court Street, Ennisicorthy 1914-1915

(Dan Walsh Collection)

County Wexford 1916 Leadership. The leading figures in a determination to rise in arms in the middle of World War One were photographed in Enniscorthy. The formal photos followed the March 1916 tour of inspection by Pádraig Pearse when the plans were formed, a date fixed and future developments estimated. This photograph was seen as an eve of national uprising sitting, the outcome of which was unknown. It was, however, expected that the planned "military manoeuvres" would be nationwide. Robert Brennan was clear that national honour demanded an armed uprising. Seated: Vice-Commandant Seamus Rafter; Robert Brennan, Brigade Quartermaster; Seamus Doyle, Brigade Adjutant; Seán Etchingham, Captain. Standing: Una Brennan, nee Bolger; Michael de Lacey and Eileen Hegarty. *(Courtesy of County Museum)*

The British Army in Ireland, 1916. C. in C. General Maxwell with his staff. From left: Capt. the Marquis of Anglesey, Brig.-Gen. Hutchinson, Capt. Bucknill, General Sir J. Maxwell, Col. Taylor, Capt. Prince Alexander of Battenberg, Gen. Byrne, and Col. Stanton.

This photograph was taken before the surrender in Enniscorthy on May 1st, 1916. Seated, Thomas Francis Meagher, Island Road; Patrick Keegan, Irish Street; Michael Davis, Shannon Hill. Standing: Michael O'Connor, John Street; Seán Gallagher, later Town Clerk.
(Photo courtesy Mary Keegan-Nolan)

Capt. Thomas Weafer.

Captain Thomas Weafer, from The Shannon in Enniscorthy, died from a sniper's bullet whilst holding the Hibernian Bank in O'Connell Street, Dublin, on April 26th, 1916. Captain Weafer belonged to E Company, 2nd Battalion, I.R.A., and was the officer in command of the detachment that escorted the lorry load of arms and stores from Fairview Park to the GPO on Easter Monday. Among the volunteers under his command on that historic occasion was his brother, Patrick, who escaped from the GPO immediately after The O'Rahilly, and, having followed him, saw him shot dead in Moore Street, a short time later.

Group of Enniscorthy Volunteers in uniform before the Rising. Front row: Seán Whelan, James Whelan. Back row: Liam Moran, Edward Nolan, Thomas Tobin.

Patrick Keegan, Irish Street, Irish Volunteer Officer, sitting in an unpretentious manner, on guard outside the premises of Capt. Seamus Rafter at the Bridge, Enniscorthy on Easter Monday 1916.

(Photo Mons. Lory Kehoe Collection)

Stanley Holloway, internationally famed stage and screen actor, star of the musical "My Fair Lady", was in the British Army at Enniscorthy in 1916.

Faced with the threat of a bombardment of the town of Enniscorthy, if the rebels would not agree to surrender, Fr. Robert Fitzhenry, Adm., urgently assembled a Peace Committee comprising a number of leading citizens. Word had soon reached the town that the insurrection had been quelled in Dublin and that Pearse had surrendered. However, the Enniscorthy leaders refused to accept the veracity of these rumours. Fr. Fitzhenry obtained their permission to travel to Wexford to seek clarification from Colonel French, the British army commander, who confirmed the reports and demanded unconditional

surrender. But this still was not acceptable to the rebel leadership, who insisted on being taken to see Pearse in person in his prison cell in Dublin. The members of the Peace Committee were: sitting, left to right – Patrick O'Neill, J.P.; Fr. Robert Fitzhenry, Canon Lyster, Church of Ireland. Standing – Patrick Byrne, J.P.; H. J. Roche, J.P.; Norman Davis, Harry Buttle.

A posed photograph of senior Volunteers. It was taken for Capt. P.P. Galligan, at Lewis Prison, England, on April 22, 1917. In front: Donnchadh O'Brien, Jas. Murphy, Thomas Doyle, Seán Moran and Séamus Moran. Back: Ed. Nolan, Edward Murphy, Michael Moran and Ted Redmond. *(Photo courtesy of Mary (Keegan) Nolan.)*

Cumann na mBan, 1916. Another group, whose names have been lost. The photograph includes four women who would have been leading members of Cumnn na mBan.

Michael O'Hanrahan, New Ross, 1916 executed leader. Michael O'Hanrahan was born on 16th March, 1877, in a house in St. Mary's Terrace which is located between South Street and Barrack Lane. Moving to Dublin with his family, he became Irish reader at the Gló Cumann Printing Works and devoted much of his spare time to journalism. He made early contact with Arthur Griffith and soon became a member of the National Council of Sinn Féin. He took part in the Easter Rising and was sentenced to death along with his brother, Henry. The latter sentence was later commuted to penal servitude for life, but Michael was executed on 4th May 1916.

At Slaney Place, Enniscorthy women and a farmer on a milk cart watch the spectacle of British artillery, possibly for the first time since June, 1798.
(Photo by courtesy Ibar Carty)

The horse-drawn artillery unit approaches Kyle Cross as two boys watch on an otherwise empty road. These photographs were taken by box camera without interference from the military.
(Tykillen Archives)

Six-horse team pulls
an artillery supply
wagon through Kyle.
(Tykillen Archives)

British artillery column at Kyle Cross on
the approach to Ferrycarrig Bridge.
(Tykillen Archives)

Men from The Milehouse and Carley's Bridge area of Enniscorthy.

ENNISCORTHY VOLUNTEERS, 1916

Among the Volunteers who took part in the 1916 Rising in Enniscorthy were men from The Milehouse and Carley's Bridge areas, two traditionally linked small settlements just outside the town. The group is shown in this photograph, possibly taken at Davis's of The Still (Fairfield).

Included in the photo are (Milehouse, except stated): Dick Foley, Davy Fenlon, Jim and Phil Redmond, Paddy Tyrell (Enniscorthy), Sam Barber, the Kenny brothers (Frank, Pearse Road, Enniscorthy, Big Joe, St. Aidan's Villas., do., and Hugh, Milehouse Road); Mogue Flood (Cherryorchard), Johnny Doyle (carpenter, Courtnacuddy, ex-Milehouse), Hall (The Still), Tim Dargan, Gallaghers, Paddy Dwyer, Marks Browne of Broomfield and Marks Browne of Bessmount, Ml, Joe Mahon, O'Neill (Cherryorchard Cross). Some of the young boys in front row include Syl Kavanagh (Carley's Bridge), Jim Doyle (The Still) and Tom Morrissey.

Photo also includes Tom Devereux of No. 4 Milehouse (second row from front, sixth from right), who played an important role in organising locals. Tom's son Paddy, who kindly loaned the photo, recalls: "My father, like most of the others involved in that period, rarely spoke to us in later years about his life as a soldier in the Boer War or taking part in the 1916 Rising. But it was people like those who were the real 'grassroots' of the country, people who were not politicians but would talk from platforms at meetings, and were also prepared to fight and give their lives for their country." An investigation into the facts surrounding the rebellion was told by R.I.C. Inspector Sharpe that there were 600 men, and 200 of them had rifles and shotguns. They established themselves in the Athenaeum as their headquarters, and appointed Irish Republican Police. They appointed sentries, and allowed no one to enter or leave the town without a permit. They commandeered motor cars, food, and every description of goods, including arms, and they searched houses for arms.

Volunteer Seán Whelan.

Seán Gallagher, Michael O'Connor, who was shot and killed at Enniscorthy Post Office, with Seán Whelan.
(Photos courtesy of Mary Farndon, Blackstoops).

An Irish volunteer with a Fianna Éireann Scout.

Volunteers Patrick Pierce, 7 St. John's Villas, Enniscorthy, and William Quirke, 1 St. John's Villas, who were appointed personal bodyguards to Pádraig Pearse when he visited Enniscorthy prior to 1916 and ended his visit by addressing a meeting in the Athenaeum. Both men were staff typographical members of Echo Newspapers and were later elected members of Enniscorthy Urban District Council.

As seen in the daily newspapers. Tom Doyle and Richard Donoghue behind prison bars. They were sent to prison in connection with the shooting of Constable Grace at Enniscorthy.

Tom Doyle, Ross Road and Richard Donohoe, Duffry Hill, Enniscorthy, being brought under military and police escort to Kilmainham Jail, 2nd May 1916. Both were sentenced to three years penal servitude.

(Photo courtesy of Liz Moorehouse).

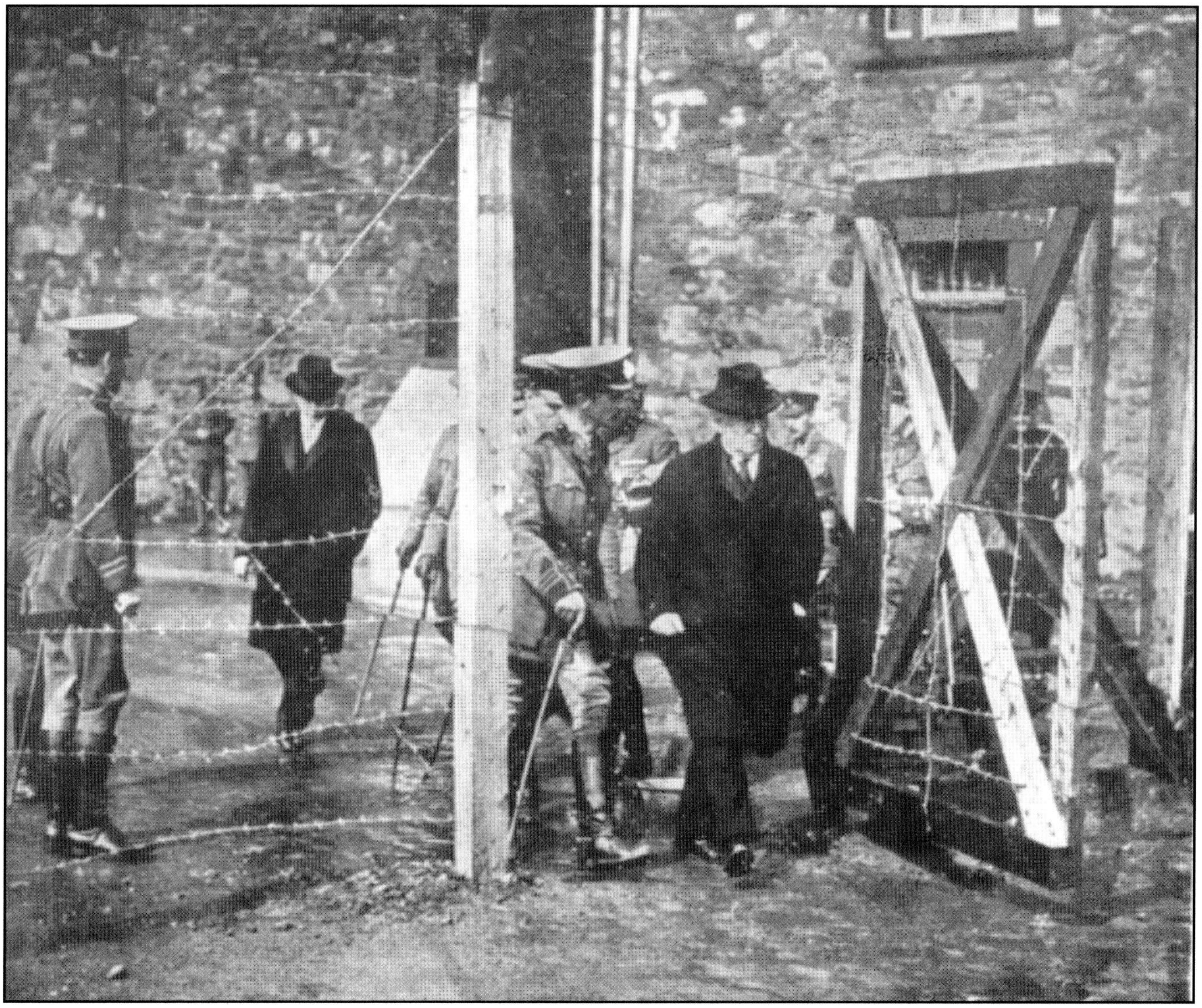

The British Prime Minister H. H. Asquith leaving Richmond Barracks where he saw some of the prisoners. *(Echo Newspapers)*

After the surrender in 1916 British soldiers were camped in Enniscorthy showgrounds and paraded to 9am Mass on Sunday mornings. This photograph shows a member of the Connaught Rangers on guard outside the cathedral.

P. H. Pearse

FIFTEEN MEN EXECUTED

(General Sir John Maxwell's Statement)

The following announcement was issued at the Irish Headquarters Command on Thursday, 11th May:

"In view of the gravity of the rebellion and its connection with German intrigue and propaganda, and in view of the great loss of life and destruction of property resulting therefrom, the General Officer Commanding-in-Chief has found it imperative to inflict the most severe sentences on the known organisers of this detestable rising and on those Commanders who took an active part in the actual fighting which occurred. It is hoped that these examples will be sufficient to act as a deterrent to intriguers, and to bring home to them that the murder of His Majesty's liege subjects, or other acts calculated to imperil the safety of the Realm will not be tolerated."

COMMANDING OFFICER'S REPORT

Confidential

From: Colonel G. A. French,
Commanding Troops,
Wexford.

To: Brigadier General,
Commanding Queenstown Garrison,
Queenstown.

Wexford May 2, 1916

Sir,

With reference to the Armed rebellion at Enniscorthy, I have the honour to report as follows.

On the evening of April 30, at 6 p.m. I held a conference at my Head Quarters to make the necessary Military arrangements to meet with the emergency in the event of either of (1) unconditional surrender or (2) refusal to surrender.

In both cases Lieutenant Colonel Digan, Commanding the Column, wished to move his force by one route and not to split it up. As I was not in possession of any accurate information as to the numbers of the insurgents or their disposition, and as a conservative estimate of the numbers was about 600 (six hundred), possibly more, with a considerable number of modern firearms, I considered that Col. Digan's proposal was reasonable and I concurred therein. I recommended his

concentrating his whole force at KILLURIN (about six miles north of Wexford), at 6.30 am May 1, whether it was either a case of surrender or no surrender. After this concentration I recommended in case of attack his moving from KILLURIN eastwards over the bridge (which together with the WEXFORD and FERRYCARRIG bridges I had held with strong military guards and barricaded since the arrival of troops at Wexford) by KYLE X roads, OYLGATE, COOLNABAY, DARBY'S GAP, BELL GRADE HOUSE, to ENNISCORTHY (reference 1" Ordnance map) taking up good gun positions for 4.7 and 18 Pr. guns as the infantry advance would ensure such positions, to bring the artillery fire on ENNISCORTHY and to shell Vinegar Hill with shrapnel. His first objectives being the destruction of the Road and Rail bridges (to cut rebel forces in two parts), the rebel strong holds in the Castle and Assembly Rooms at ENNISCORTHY. It was my intention in the event of attack to have remained with Lieutenant Colonel Digan throughout, and, should circumstances so warrant, to assume command myself as I had previously informed your General Staff Officer by telephone.

In the event of surrender I left the advance into ENNISCORTHY in the hands of Lieutenant Colonel Digan, but recommended his adhering to the route laid down for attack, as that roadway was clear of trees and other barricades and obstructions. I, however, stipulated that all the usual military precautions should be taken and not to place too much reliance on freedom from attack.

On April 30, as you were informed by telephone, two rebel leaders were despatched by Motor to Dublin to consult with Pearse (their imprisoned leader). They returned here about 7.30 p.m. same date, and I gave them till midnight to notify me the decision arrived at by the rebels at ENNISCORTHY. At midnight, April 30, May 1, a deputation arrived from ENNISCORTHY (headed by Fr. Fitzhenry as head of Peace Mission but not associated with the rebel movement in any way) bearing a despatch stating that 4 leaders would surrender, but requesting that the rank and file should be spared. To this I replied that the surrender must be unconditional and the surrender of 6 leaders (whose names I know) would be insisted upon, and that their followers would also be arrested either at once or rounded up later. I also stipulated that all arms and warlike material were to be surrendered, stolen and looted property returned without delay, and all barricades and obstacles removed. I also informed the peace deputation that in the event of the troops being fired upon by any of the insurgents extreme measures would be immediately adopted. The deputation stated that it would do its best to ensure the fulfilment of unconditional surrender and the other conditions, but doubted whether the leaders could prevail upon their followers to give themselves up. As however the names of most of their followers were known to the police I did not consider their immediate surrender imperative.

The deputation informed me, however, that it would do its best in this respect and would endeavour to see that the six leaders surrendered at once. It returned to ENNISCORTHY about 1 a.m. May 1, and I instructed Lieutenant Colonel Digan to march on ENNISCORTHY on the Surrender basis. I directed him to time his march so that the troops would actually be marching through the town at the hour I had arranged to make the arrests. The infantry (which were encamped 3 miles to the South of Wexford). I told Lieutenant Colonel Digan to move by rail WEXFORD to KILLURIN and I instructed the railway authorities to this effect.

On May 1, accompanied by District Inspector O'Hara, R.I.C., and Colonel Jameson Davis, Commanding National Volunteers Co. Wexford, I motored direct to ENNISCORTHY without molestation in any way, and there found that the Armoured train was at the station, the damage to the railway having proved trifling and easily repairable by the R.E. Detachment with the train. I commandeered the sports field for accommodation of the troops, ascertained that the 6 rebel leaders were awaiting arrest at Assembly Rooms, but that their followers had vanished (the bulk having come in from the surrounding country) and taken all modern rifles with them. Steps are, however, being taken to locate these arms and it is anticipated that a number will shortly be rounded up. I then awaited the arrival of the column, and as soon as it had entered the town I arrested the leaders, took possession of the Assembly rooms, and collected arms, explosives, etc. (vido list attached). By arresting the leaders whilst the troops were marching through the attention of the crowd and sympathisers was distracted and the arrest was quietly effected. I despatched the prisoners to Wexford by Motors under Armed guard, and at 7.45 a.m. this morning they wee railed to Waterford in charge of District Inspector O'Hara, R.I.C.

The troops were well received on the whole, but it is apparent that there are large numbers of the populace with Sinn Fein sympathies.

The following points I wish to bring to notice:

(a) That the damage to property was not extensive, and on the whole the insurgents were, generally speaking, well behaved. All the public houses were closed and there were only a few reports of the use of firearms, notably two cases, viz. that a firing on Dr.

Furlong and the R.I.C. Barracks, one Constable wounded but the number of shots fired at the Barrack could not have been numerous as evidenced by the windows and wall of the building. Several telegraph poles were cut down.

(b) It is essential that the "Echo" newspaper should be suppressed. This paper is responsible for much of the Sinn Fein movement in the town. This I have learned by reports received from trustworthy sources.

(c) There was a certain amount of looting and commandeering of food, bedding, arms, etc. in the town, but not to any very serious extent. There were, however, numerous cases of Motor cars, etc. being forcibly commandeered both in the town and a radius of about 7 miles. There were also some cases of looting cattle and sheep by the insurgents for food, notably one case at OULART.

(d) I consider that it would be advisable to retain the column despatched under Lieutenant Colonel Digan within the County of Wexford for some time (less the 4.7 gun and armoured train) with its Head Quarters at ENNISCORTHY and sending out flying columns therefrom as I may direct. The present garrison of Wexford should remain for some considerable time until the bulk of the arrests have been effected and the district has resumed its normal peaceful state.

(e) I will arrange strong patrols combined of both military and R.I.C. proceeding by motor from Wexford to all outlying disaffected areas and will in most cases accompany same myself. I intend to have all troops, both those at Wexford and Enniscorthy very much in evidence, and will arrange accordingly. I, of course, assume that I can instruct O.C. Troops, Enniscorthy to supply such flying columns, etc. as I consider necessary, and that he is under my orders whilst within the County of Wexford.

I have the honour to be Sir,
Your obedient servant,
Colonel Commanding Troops,
Wexford

List of Arms, etc. seized at Enniscorthy on 1st May, 1916 and now stored in police Barrack, South Main Street, Wexford

No.	Description of Arms	No. of Arms	Remarks
1.	Guns and rifles	21	
2.	Pikes	60	
3.	Pikes having handles	6	
4.	Tins of Petrol	15	

List of Ammunition, etc. seized at Enniscorthy on 1st May, 1916, and now stored in R.I.C. Barracks, Enniscorthy.

No.	Description of Ammunition	Number of, or amount	Remarks
1.	Coils of Fuse	56	
2.	Sporting Cartridges	53 stone	
3.	Blasting Powder	30 stone	
4.	Shot	10 stone	
5.	Gunpowder	2 stone	
6.	Ammunition for Revolver and Rifle	4,000 rounds	
7.	Bombs	1	
8.	Telephone Apparatus	1	

Prisoners in Stafford Prison June 1916 including James Ryan, T. Ennis and Murt O'Connell

Easily identifiable amongst the returned prisoners on board the carriage is Robert Brennan with his convict cap and number 103. The procession is preceeded by the tricolour.

LETTER FROM MOUNTJOY

Typed from handwritten letter:
Mountjoy Prison 31-5-16

My dear Jim

It is not very often you will have such a surprise as to hear from <u>me</u> from Mountjoy and indeed I suppose I should not write to you at all only to report that there is nothing new here in Ireland. Everything is new alas! at present. No one could have foreseen a little while ago the Ireland of today – at least <u>one</u> Ireland of today. I presume there are some people untouched even by the present catastrophe.

I need not tell you what is common knowledge now – all about the Rising. But I do ask you to take the trouble to find out all about it & perhaps you can as easily as I, given from various sources – its origin, aim, result in public opinion in Ireland, <u>first and now,</u> and in other countries, and for the sake of old times.

Don't read the stupid Wexford papers on it; they are imbecile. I will tell you about ourselves.

First I must say I have many, many dear friends who have suffered the varying penalties – even the extreme penalty – & some whose fate is not decided yet? Notably Agnes' fiance & many other great friends. There are only 12 women under arrest in all Ireland now. We are in jail about a month now. Myself and Nell and Kathleen Browne, Bridgetown are 3 of them. The other 9 are Dublin women, all well known tho' I don't think you know any of them. Jim is in an English Detention Barrack like thousands of others – so is Paddy Kehoe and probably some of your football friends. I don't think you know the Dublin people we know there. Those most obviously criminally implicated have been tried and sentenced – others taken in the rank and file fight or as suspects connected with the movement or volunteers who did not fight have been shipped off to these detention barracks; their status is not yet defined. A good many are still here in Richmond awaiting further orders. We (women) have also received Deportation orders to an internment barrack in England or to any one of a no. of spots selected as places of residence for us there. We prefer the latter and it might prove expensive if we were forgotten there. I earned between £400 & £450 last year. If I lose that, I shall find such a project very expensive. Of course, there has been a great deal of protest against us (women) being deported and we half hope we may not have to go at all.

I don't know what will happen to me in the university. The students are so enthusiastically excited over me that I think the authorities don't want me back just yet at all events. I shall have to emigrate or do as many or most of my sex do so eventually late as it is! I was at home for Easter when the Rising broke out in Dublin. (In Enniscorthy too, but no fighting. Nothing in Wexford town).

Naturally I was arrested immediately I got back. My house here was searched for hours I was taken to Kilmainham and thence here. Nell was arrested in Wexford. Jim had been in England a week when I got to Dublin. First it was awful; no one knew where anyone was.

Wexford would really sicken you when I was there. I believe things have changed. Not that there were not some what one calls <u>decent</u> people, first or last. From reports I believe (I don't know personally) the two houses in law of yours (I mean in which your cousins reside) represented the opposite extremes in sentiment.

I wonder was it a pity you were not in Ireland this year? How changed since you were here and perhaps changes coming, whoever will enjoy them. My friends have been splendid. It is like a theatre, people going to see prisoners in Dublin. I hope to, for I shall be in 19 Ranelagh Road if you write soon again. I have a lease on the house.

Your friend

Mary K. Ryan

(Mary Kate Ryan was of the Tomcoole family, Taghmon, a highly qualified academic. She became the first wife of Seán T. O'Kelly. She died rather young and Sean T. later President of Ireland, married her sister Phyllis. The Jim referred to in her letter is her brother, Dr. James Ryan, later Cabinet Minister and Tanaiste, Nell is her sister, remembered as a trenchant Fianna Fáil, long serving member of Wexford County Council. Agnes is another sister of the writer, engaged to Denis McCullough, Belfast, President of the Irish Republican Brotherhood, whom she later married. Paddy Kehoe of Glencarraig, Enniscorthy is referred to. He was one of the most dominant and self-sacrificing motivators in the National movement. It is understood that the letter was written to a friend in Australia.

Photo taken by Murt O'Connell at Stafford Prison, England, July 1916. Medical student James Ryan of Tomcoole is third from right.

County Wexford prisoners in Stafford Jail, June 1916.

Football team in
Stafford Prison, 1916.
Note the smiling British
soldiers, guards
presumably, at either
side of the team.

18th May, 1916.

Dear Colonel French,

      Needless to say I was very gratified to receive your letter of today's date, intimating your pleasure at the attitude of the Citizens of Wexford during the recent deplorable disturbances.

      I have taken the liberty to send your letter to the local Press, as I am aware that the townspeople will very much appreciate your allusions to their action during the crisis, now happily at an end.

      I am sure that it is unnecessary for me to add that you may always rely on Wexfordmen doing their utmost to uphold the good name of the town in every way possible, and that the vast majority of them will ever be found on the side of law and order.

      May I add a word of praise as to the manner in which the Troops under your Command carried out their various duties during the critical times of the past few weeks.

Colonel G. A. French,

    Commanding Troops,

      Co. Wexford.

Yours very truly,

Nicholas Byrne

Mayor of Wexford.

GRATIFICATION

ESMONDE'S PROTEST

TO THE EDITOR OF THE LONDON MORNING POST

SIR, I have grown sick and tired of the incessant abuse of Ireland in connection with the war. I do not know if there is any sense of fair-play left in England where Ireland is concerned, but if there is the interests both of the war and of the Empire would suggest a stop to this unending vilification of Irishmen. Neither do I know if there is anyone in England of sufficient manliness and honesty and authority to cry halt to this hideous campaign of hate. It would be to England's interest if he could be speedily discovered.

What have we Irish done already in this war? We have supported it from the outset. We have done all we could to ensure its success in the teeth of the bitterest official opposition in every quarter. We have submitted to the ghastly misgovernment of our country and to all the needless vexations of so-called war measures without protest. We have contributed far more than our fair share of war taxation without complaint. We have sent the flower of our manhood to fight and die without either reward or recognition. We have done all this, first, because we believed in the justice of the war; and secondly, because we believed in the promises of English statesmen. The character of the war remains the same, but through monstrous mismanagement it has brought us infinitely greater sorrow and loss than we ever could have anticipated.

The promises of English statesmen turn out to be scraps of paper, and what do we Irish get in return for our sacrifices? Nothing but abuse, gross, cowardly and dishonest abuse. When I think of our glorious regiments and their unacknowledged deeds of unsurpassed heroism, of our gallant Irish sailors who for two terrible years have guarded the Empire in stress and storm and danger from the Arctic to the Antarctic; when I think of Flanders and France, and Gallipoli, and Serbia, and Mesopotamia, and Egypt, of the landing at the Dardanelles with its awful toll of Irish lives, of our splendid 10th Irish Division recklessly thrown away by British incompetency, of the hundreds of Irish sailors who perished in the Jutland Battle, 300 of them in two ships alone; and when I think of our desolate Irish homes, of the unnumbered Irish fathers and mothers and sons and daughters who have bravely and uncomplainingly given what they loved best on earth to the service of the Empire, I ask myself what spirit possesses the anti-Irish when not even our children's sacrifice will propitiate them. —Yours, etc, THOS. H. GRATTAN ESMONDE. House of Commons, August 18th 1916.

Editor's reply

Sir Thomas Esmonde's tirade is based on a monstrous mis-statement of the facts. There has been no lack of recognition of the splendid qualities of the Irish soldiers and sailors; and where there has been mis-management it is not, as he suggests, the Irish who have solely or even mainly suffered. Yet the others do not upbraid. The "hideous campaign of hate" of which he speaks is a figment of his imagination, in spite of the provocation some of Mr. Dillon's speeches have given. But the British nation would be more than human if it could forget that the Irish people, alone in the United Kingdom, have refused obligatory military service; and that, in the crisis of the war, a section of the Irish people tried to stab this country in the back by rising in rebellion. If the lives of those who have been needlessly sacrificed are to be counted we must not forget the devoted Sherwood Foresters in Dublin. Editor, M.P.

International reaction to the events and executions in 1916 was angry. Exiles were outraged everywhere in the world. This reaction had greater significance in the United States which Britain anxiously wished to involve in the war on their side. Urgent pressure from America forced Britain to release all the 1916 prisoners between Christmas 1916 and June 1917. Our photograph shows the first batch arriving at Westland Row (now Pearse) Station at Christmas 1916.

Robert Brennan, convict.

Public feeling after the executions changed into veneration for the fallen leaders and support for the families of the dead. The surviving volunteers in Dublin and Enniscorthy were regarded as audacious heroes. Ireland was changed in a way which was as surprising as it was swift. The elderly Redmonds saw the fabric of their ambitions and life's work undermined. The 1916 rising and its grim aftermath destroyed John Redmond's political base. The Irish National Party, of which he was the leader, was abandoned. His members of parliament had also been horrified at the protracted executions and the numbers executed. The nationalist Irish people saw in Sinn Féin their best prospect. In June 1917 all the prisoners had been released and welcomed home with comprehensive celebration.

The Band of the Wexford Militia taken around 1900 in Wexford Military Barracks. The Wexford militia was the Third Militia Battalion, Royal Irish Regiment. That was the units definition since 1818 when Cardwell's Territorial Organisation came into force. The militia units were a paid part-time service usually intended to aid the civil authorities in phases of turbulence. Some members of this unit signed for overseas service which meant a few shillings more monthly. They did so in the understandable belief that they would never be called upon. A big mistake. When the Boer War in South Africa turned against the British regular army many of them were called up for service out on the Veldt.

(Courtesy Journal Wexford Historical Society)

THE
ENTERTAINMENT TRADITION

1913: The Athenaeum Choral and Dramatic Operatic Society of Enniscorthy under the inspiration of magnificent Chevalier Grattan Flood, historian and musician, chose and produced a sophisticated French musical "La Fille de Madam Angot".

The cast photograph of a 1912 Presentation Convent Schools, Wexford play dates from 1911-12. It is obviously about the early Christian martyrs in Imperial Rome, a typical school theme at the time. They were soon to be replaced by Irish Ireland themes, Gaelic mythology and plays by Pádraig Pearse. The only faces we can identify with certainty are the shield and sword holder at extreme right, Johanna (Joey) Doyle, Talbot Street, and third from right, front row, Therese Gaul, Gaul Hardware and Undertakers, South Main Street (now Penneys). The identity of the executioner with (presumably) a Gaul axe, must remain a deep mystery. *(Photo by Charles Vize, courtesy of Eamon Doyle)*

In a long County Wexford tradition Enniscorthy's Mental Hospital band, composed of brasses and stringed instruments, present themselves to the public in 1900. They last played in a public procession in 1926. *(Ann Marsh Collection)*

Ferns Dramatic Society presented "The Irishman" on stage on 9, 12 and 16 September 1917. The same play was also performed in Ferns in 1898. Back row: Wally Barnes, Martin Dunbar, Matt Murphy, Patsy McCullough, George Butler, Jimmy Doyle, Tommy Whelan, Owen Sheridan. Standing: Andy Breslin, Tommy Nolan, Dick Redmond, Thady Bolger, Ned Nangle, Michael Maguire, John Pender, Jim Treacy, Henry Kehoe, Thomas Bookey. Seated: Mrs Sarah Kehoe, Jim Breslin, Lizzie Sheridan, Rev. Richard Gaul, Ms. Donnelly, May Butler, William Nangle. Front row: Mr. Pender, Pat Doyle, Owen Redmond.

The Gorey Musicians were to the fore in the revival of the "War Pipes." In 1912 a newly-formed pipe band helped the republican movement. Its members and their families suffered for playing at Sinn Féin meetings. Their proudest possession was a beautiful flag, seen in the photo, presented to them by Mr. F. J. Biggar, Belfast, in the Bullring, Wexford in 1913.
(Michael Fitzpatrick Collection)

The anti-recruiting song contributed by the late Mike Nolan of John Street, Enniscorthy, was sung at a concert in the Athenaeum by a singer named Mulkerns. He was known as "The Rajah of Frongoch" (Jail, 1916). Another singer was the later famed Gerard Crofts who had contacted eczema in both hands while in Wandsworth prison. It was widely sung from 1917 until the conscription threat from the British Government passed.

As I was walking down the street,
  Feeling fine and larky O,
A recruiting sergeant I did meet –
  Said he you'd look fine in khaki O
.
The King, you see, is wanting men,
  Just read this proclamation O,
The time 'tis good, for you 'twill be,
  A jolly fine vacation O.

"That may be true," I answered back,
  "But tell me, sergeant dearie, O,

If I had a pack upon my back,
  Would I be feeling cheery O?
I'd have to drill and train until
  They made me one of the Frenchies O."

The sergeant swung his little cane,
  His smile was most provoking O.
He curled his little muss again,
  Said he "you're only joking O.
The sandbags are so nice and high,
  The wind you won't feel blowing O."
I winked at someone passing by,
  Said I "It might be snowing O."

So hail or rain or hottest sun,
  I'm not going out to Flanders O,
There's work in Ireland to be done,
  While you send out your ganders O.
Let Englishmen for England fight,
  Tis nearly time they started, O,"
I bade the sergeant brave goodnight,
  And after that we parted O.

Loughnageer Mummers, 1914 - 1916. Back, left to right: Dick Nugent, Tommy Miskella, Mick Quinn, Aidan Cullen, Bob Cahill and Tommy Cullen. Front: Dick Murphy, Luke Murphy, Larry Crowley, Jim Cullen and Jimmy Miskella. Photo by Nicholas Cullen.
(James Parle Collection)

Art MacMurrough's war pipe band, Enniscorthy 1920. This is a fine photograph but unfortunately all record of the band's activities and their names appear to be lost. *(Dan Walsh Collection)*

Irish National Foresters' Brass and Reed Band 1917. Pictured outside the Foresters' Rooms in Court Street are, back row: L.J. Lynch, T. Driscoll, D. O'Farrell, F. Murphy, M. Sullivan, E. Somers, J.McCarthy, J. Gerathy, P. Dunne. Front row: M. Maguire, T. Coghlan, J. Wickham, P. Murphy, D. O'Connor, M. Somers, J. Moran and, seated, J.J. Somers and J.Coghlan. *(Courtesy Dan Walsh)*

The de Lacy band,
founded 1908.

This unusual musical family, "The de Lacys" from Ferns, were frequent visitors to Gorey during the 1913-1920 era. The Gorey Trade and Labour Pipe Band was organised at that time and both bands had a lot in common. The deLacy band suffered the loss of their instruments and uniforms, when their home was destroyed by fire. The parents were Michael and Elizabeth de Lacy whose children and grandchildren became accomplished musicians and members of Comhaltas Ceóltoiri Éireann.

(Michael Fitzpatrick Collection)

The Gorey Trade and Labour Band, circa 1912-1920. Front row: Michael Jackman and J. Tompkins. Second row; Peter Connelly, Jack Walker, Eddie McDonagh, Darby O'Neill, Moses Robinson, Jimmy Berry, Bob Duncan, Jack Breen, Enniscorthy, Joe Clarke. Back row: James Cleeson, Seán O'Byrne, Wm. Keegan.
(Michael FitzPatrick Collection)

The Bread and Porter Band. The photo from an anonymous donor comes to us without names. This war pipes, fife and drum band was the band formed at the end of World War One in Wexford by Wexfordmen who had served in the Boer War and World War One. In the latter's cruel waste of youth and life it was proposed to their belief that they were fighting for the freedom of small nations like Belgium and for the 32-County Home-Rule Ireland of John Redmond, little aware that their ideal was already undermined. The branch of Wexford's British Legion of ex-servicemen was named after the middle-aged national party hero, Major Willie Redmond, who had been killed on the western front following a gesture of rash heroism unequalled in war. He was 57 when he joined the Irish regiments. The flags on either side of the door are the old flags of nationalist Ireland, on the right the green with the harp and on the left the sunburst emblem. The band was known in Wexford as "The Bread and Porter Band".

The Presentation Convent School, Wexford, rises to the occasion as it did annually, despite dungeon, fire and sword. Is this wartime all-girls show "The Pirates of Penzance?". We can't say for sure, but there is a fearsome pirate king with broad sword and the two scoundrels smoking pipes alongside him look up to no good. The girls look terrified and why wouldn't they be when moustached scoundrels are taken into account.

The Wexford St. Patrick's Fife and Drum Band as it was in 1926. Back row (left to right): Kevin Rossiter, Willie Hore, Fintan Morris, James Bergin, Willie Morris, Pat Hore, Lar Cleary, Moses O'Leary, Tom Brennan, Martin Stafford. Second row: Toddy Rossiter, Aidan O'Keeffe, Tom Hore, Mikie O'Neill, Frank Kehoe, Michael Stafford, Mick Morris, Davy Morris, Peter Rutttedge. Third row: Fran Rossiter, Paddy Cleary, Dan Bergin, Micky Culleton, William Devereux, John Leary, Ned Nolan, James Phillips. Fourth row: Tommy Morris, Michael O'Neill, Mick Sutherland, Mickey Kehoe, James Neill. Front: Michael Sutherland, Johnny Kehoe, Aidan Hore, Patty Sutherland, John Sutherland and John O'Brien.

Saltmills Mummers c.1924. Exhaustive enquiries have failed to identify any member of this fine set. (Valentine Molloy, b. 1906 says they are before his time). Jack and Willie Clarke are probably included.

(James Parle Collection)

Life carried on despite the ferocity of the Civil War bitterness. For school children it was a grown-ups war; but all carried the influences of heated discussions in their homes and outside. The Franciscan Fathers in Wexford produced an entertainment in 1923 and involved their junior choirs and altar boys. Accuracy in identification presents an almost insurmountable problem but there are at least personalities whose extraordinary influence carried on down to the 1970s and beyond. Seated between the two Franciscans is Mary Codd who devoted and sacrificed her life to music, choral, voice, stage and orchestral art in County Wexford. The gentleman at extreme left is journalist and musician Thomas Fane, Taghmon who later became editor of The People Group of Newspapers, Wexford. In the seated row amongst the orchestra members, fourth from left, is Bessie O'Connor of the North Main Street confectionary, a member of an active nationalist family, an enthusiastic supporter of the arts, Wexford Festival Opera and Historical Society. Kneeling in the front row, at extreme left in short pants, is Nicholas Fennell of a very musical family. The boy sitting in front at extreme right is John "Sandy" Walsh of Wygram, later John "Welsh" the actor on stage, screen and television in London for decades. Also in front is his brother Tom, later founder of the Wexford Festival Opera. Tom was older then "Sandy" so we suspect, repeat, suspect, that he is the boy fourth from Sandy's left. In the back row, sixth from left, is Patricia Furlong, daughter of Mattie, the outspoken businessman and committed Irish Irelander of South Main Street. Third from right, back row, is the famed contralto and recording artiste Nellie Walsh, sister of Sandy and Tom. The gentleman at extreme right is theatre expert Michael O'Neill of Selskar.

Seated in the "senior" middle row, third from right, is Mae Samson whose family had a quality butchers shop opposite White's Hotel. Next to her is Mae Morrissey, niece of the foundry owning nationalist Doyle Brothers of Redmond Square. Alongside Mae is Margaret Leacy, Westlands. The Franciscan Father to her right is Fr. Stanislaus who was one of the most popular friars to serve in Wexford. The other Franciscan is unidentified but alongside him is a long serving choir member, Mrs. Paul Roche, whose husband was manager of The People Newspapers Group.

The small girl in front of Thomas Fane is Emily O'Loughlin. The girl at extreme left in the back row is her sister, Lily. The musical play was called "Slumberland".

WAR OFF THE WEXFORD COAST

World War One lapped against Wexford's Atlantic and Irish Sea shores. Germany's U-boats infested the waters around Tuskar Rock, The Hook and the Saltee Islands. At the time, Liverpool was the major British port for transatlantic shipping. Southampton had yet to be developed. The sea route, therefore, with supplies from America passed Wexford's coast. All the German U-boats had to do was to lie in wait. The most active of these U-boats was the U20 under the command of Kapitan-Leutnant Walter Schwieger. Schwieger had G type torpedoes, which were extremely unreliable (he did not even expect the torpedo to sink the ship, only to see what damage it did). During World War One, several thousand ships were sunk by U-boats alone.

In February 1915 the German Government declared a policy of attacking and sinking any ships found within a stated blockade zone, which surrounded Britain and Ireland. They further declared that while all efforts would be made not to sink neutral vessels their safety could not be guaranteed within that area. Notices were run in American papers warning that ships sporting the British flag risked attack and destruction.

Lusitania

Finally, on 7th May 1915, the almost inevitable result of such a policy occurred. A Cunard cruise ship, allegedly with munitions on board, Lusitania, was torpedoed and sunk just off the Irish coast. Of the 2,000 people aboard, 1,200 were drowned, including 128 neutral Americans.

The U-boat responsible was U20.

Schweiger received the Iron Cross from an unrepentant High Command for his sinking of the ship. During the next year he steadily increased his personal score, affirming his position as one of Germany's new U-boat aces. Schweiger later went on to command the newer U88, adding to his tally. After 12 operational patrols Schweiger had sunk 190,000 tons of enemy shipping, becoming the seventh highest scoring German U-boat commander of World War One, though probably the most notorious.

Inventor

The new role of the submarine in warfare was so dominant that the name of that craft's inventor is worthy of mention. He was John Philip Holland (1840-1914) who, as Brother Holland, had taught in the Christian Brothers School in Enniscorthy. Holland began work on the idea of a submarine while teaching school from 1858 to 1872. He left for the United States in 1873 and after many years of failures he eventually succeeded and the US government awarded him the contract to build a submarine. He died in poverty following the collapse of his company.

The British navy, army and air corps tried to overcome the crippling losses off Wexford's coasts in several ways. They installed a sonar underwater detection base at 'Four Winds House', Saint Helen's, Rosslare, and they had an airship base in the wooded surroundings of Johnstown Castle.

Airships

Airships were invented by Count Ferdinand von Zeppelin. He was born July 8, 1838, in Konstanz, Prussia. He entered the Prussian army in 1858. Zeppelin went to the United States in 1863 to work as a military observer for the Union army in the American Civil War, making his first balloon flight while he was in Minnesota. The Royal Air Corps' airships were inadequate to deal with the U-boats campaign. Until 1918, the last year of the World War, it was feared that the U-boats alone had the capability of forcing Britain to commence peace negotiations.

John Holland, inventor of the submarine, emerges from a proto model in a U.S. Naval base. The submarine warfare off Wexford's coast was not the only connection. As Brother John Holland he taught in the Christian Brothers School in Enniscorthy. He died in 1914 without seeing the awesome result of his genius. He was 73 years of age. An Post, the Irish Post Office, issued a special commemorative stamp in his honour in 1981. The United States Post Master General had a stamp issued in Holland's honour in 2000.

The once isolated house at bleak St. Helen's, known as "The Four Winds." Situated near the entrance to the Irish Sea from the Atlantic, it was a Royal Navy sonar submarine detection base in World War One when the U-boat successes were at their height. The commanding Royal Navy officer was Captain Herbert George Davis. His family kept coming back for holidays and eventually bought the adjacent land. Captain Davis' grand-daughter, Jill, married the outstanding All-Ireland medal winning hurler, Billy Rackard. The land now forms part of St. Helen's Golf Club.

Royal Flying Corps airship, secure and snug in its moorings in the wood beside the lake in Johnstown Castle. The commanding officer in Johnstown was H. L. Fuller who later lived in Arran Lodge, Crossabeg. In 1917 he became liaison officer between the R.F.C. and the American Naval Airforce newly based at Ferrybank, Wexford. Mrs. Fuller became an enthusiastic member of the Wexford Historical Society. Her niece, Felicity Lambert of Coolballow, married Captain John Poole of Ballyfinogue, later commodore of Irish Shipping.

Royal Flying Corps airship flies gently southwards towards the U-boat infested Atlantic approaches. Kelly's Hotel Rosslare guests could watch and take photos at their ease.
(Nicholas Kelly photograph)

Royal Flying Corps airship returns to base in Johnstown Castle. Its leisurely pace enabled photos to be taken by simple cameras. This photo was taken from the home of M. J. O'Connor, solr. in Westlands, Wexford

The airships that operated from their base at Johnstown Castle were sometimes called Zepplins, after the retired army officer, Count von Zeppelin, who pioneered this type of craft in Germany in 1898. It was so successful that the Kaiser decorated Zepplin with the Order of the Black Eagle. Zeppelin formed a commercial company, and between 1910 and 1914, it built a succession of rigid airships which, in that period, carried over 17,000 passengers and flew 100,00 miles without one fatality.

In 1909 British public opinion, becoming alarmed at the disparity between Germany and England, induced the government to take action and the British Admiralty undertook the production of a rigid airship, and a contract was placed with Messrs Vickers Ltd to built "Naval Airship Bo. 1", subsequently called the "Mayfly".

This airship was intended to fulfil the duties of an aerial scout and to be capable of maintaining a speed of 40 knots for, if possible, 24 hours. She was to moor by the nose to a post on the water (or possibly on land also).

Royal Flying Corps airships.

Royal Flying Corp airship operating out of Johnstown Castle grounds, the S.S.Z. 37, overflying a U.S. Navy sloop in 1917 near Tuskar Rock.

Royal Flying Corps bomber aims manually at a submarine from his airship.

The German Zeppelins were used for passenger transport as well as for military purposes. After the outbreak of the World War One, the German military made extensive use of Zeppelins as bombers and scouts, but were not notably successful. At the beginning of the conflict the German command had high hopes for the craft, as they appeared to have compelling advantages over contemporary aircraft - they were almost as fast, carried many more guns, and had a greater bomb load capacity and enormously greater range and endurance, but their great weakness was their vulnerability to gunfire.

The first offensive use of Zeppelins was just two days after the invasion of Belgium. A single craft, the Z J[7]/, was damaged by gunfire and made a forced landing near Cologne. Two more Zeppelins were shot down in August and one was captured by the French. Their use against well-defended targets in daytime raids was a mistake and the High Command lost all confidence in the Zeppelin, leaving it to the Naval Air Service to make any further use of the craft.

During the entire war around 1,200 scouting flights were made. The Naval Air Service also directed a number of strategic raids against Britain, leading the way in bombing techniques and also forcing the British to bolster their anti-aircraft defences. The first airship raids were approved by the Kaiser in January 1915. The nighttime raids were intended to target only military sites.

THE U-BOAT WAR

The name of Liverpool crops up with regularity in the records of torpedoed ships. In 1915, particularly when it became evident that a land war of attrition was being waged by the generals with no immediate end in sight, the U-boat campaign against Allied shipping of every kind intensified. On March 17 the Booth Lines "S.S. Anthony" of Liverpool was torpedoed south of the Hook Lighthouse while homeward bound from Para via Lisbon with the loss of fifty lives.

On the 25th of April 1915 Fregattenkapitan (Commander) Herman Bauer of the 3rd Submarine Flotilla ordered U-20 and U-27 to the Irish Sea and Bristol Channel. U-20 was commanded by Kaptianleutnant Walther Schwieger, a successful and popular commander. She sailed from Emden on 30 April. On the morning of the 6 May at 07:40 Schwieger met the Harrison Line steamer *Centurian*, 5,945 tons, thirteen miles southeast of Coningbeg Light. He opened up with guns, then allowed the crew to escape after the ship hove-to. The ship was outward bound from Liverpool to Durban, South Africa, with 9,000 tons of general cargo. The 44-man crew took to two of the ship's boats but decided to return to their vessel when she appeared to be remaining afloat. They were then approached by the submarine and ordered to keep clear as another torpedo was fired and sank the ship. In the afternoon at 14:30 U-20 spotted *Candidate*, another Harrison Line ship, about seventeen miles south of the lightship: Schwieger torpedoed her without warning. The 44-man crew of the 5,858 ton *Candidate* were rescued by the steam trawler *Lord Allendale*. She then chased the collier *Olivia* on passage from Newport to Waterford, but the vessel escaped. On Friday 7 May 1915, U-20 was off the Old Head of Kinsale and she met the Cunard Liner *Lusitania*. On the understanding that she carried munitions she was torpedoed by the U-20. This was the greatest and most infamous wartime tragedy in Irish waters. Some 1200 men, women and children were lost. It was used to create a devastating world opinion of German tactics and was said to have greatly influenced the move towards entering the war by the United States. The U-20 also sank the *Hesperian*, 10,920 tons, off the Fastnet on 4-9-1914 with the loss of 32 lives, and the *Cymric*, 13,370 tons, on the 8th May 1915 with the loss of five lives. The U-20 went ashore and was scuttled off Denmark in 1917 and Captain Schwieger took command of U-88.

Kapitan-Leutnant Walter Schwieger Commander of the U.20

The German Navy U (Unterzeeboot) Boat U.20 which operated off the Wexford and Waterford coasts.

An unidentified U-boat off the Wexford coast preparing to fire, almost certainly in practice.
(Duncannon Fort Maritime Museum Collection)

A British tanker after a direct hit.

Following the sinking of the Lusitania the propaganda opportunity was seized instantly by Britain's War Office. Ireland was specifically targeted because conscription did not obtain there. It is significant that the appeals were directed at potential volunteers for the army regiments and not the Royal Navy.

The U.44, sunk south-west of the Hook on 15 August, 1917, was raised with great effort by Royal Navy divers and their latest equipment off the coast floor. It was towed to Dunmore East as seen in our photograph, thoroughly examined for the up-to-date German technology developments, taken back to sea and scuttled. The captain was the only one of the U.44 crew to survive and report details of the disaster. *(Photo by courtesy of John Power).*

The art of persuading men to enlist in all the contending armies intensified as the war became grimmer and seemingly intractable. The propaganda efforts to recruit Irish soldiers used emotional, patriotic, challenging, bravery and "fighting Irish" appeal to save "small nations", i.e. Belgium (of the massive, brutally administered Congo African Empire). The posters used in war propaganda in Ireland were masters of the recruitment sergeant's art. This was particularly important in Ireland where the proposal to introduce conscription was resolutely opposed. The sinking of the Lusitania was used to influence America's entrance into the war. As this poster showed, the German, a darkly coloured jungle beast, was presented as fit for extermination.

The S.S. "Feltria" torpedoed by U.C48 off Mine Head on May 5, 1917.
(Duncannon Fort Maritime Museum Collection)

S.S. "Barrister" taking water. Torpedoed and sunk seven miles off Mine Head on May 11, 1917.

The S.S. "Greta" sunk in May 1917 by UC48 11 miles South East of Mine Head.
(Duncannon Fort Maritime Musuem Collection)

The S.S. "Carlow" torpedoed and sunk by U.95 seven miles south west of the Conningbeg Lightship.
(Duncannon Fort Maritime Museum Collection)

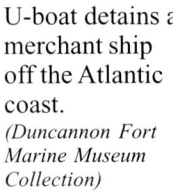

U-boat detains a merchant ship off the Atlantic coast.
(Duncannon Fort Marine Museum Collection)

The S.S. "Artist" torpedoed off the Hook on January 27, 1917.
(Duncannon Fort Maritime Musuem Collection)

The S.S. "Mesaba" torpedoed off the Tuskar Rock, September 1, 1915.
(Duncannon Fort Maritime Museum Collection)

WOUNDED AT GALLIPOLI

Abraham Dixon of the well-known Wexford seafaring family of William St. House, a family widely connected in Wexford history for centuries. Prior to going to the United States in 1923 he had been with the Limerick Steamship Company and served throughout the 1914-1918 war on the Leyland Company's ships. An engineer, he served his apprenticeship with Vickers-Armstrong and worked building machinery for submarines. He took part in several submarine trials. While serving at sea he found himself and his ship involved in the ill-fated landings by British and colonial forces at Gallipoli in Turkey. Our photo donor, Mary Corcoran, informs us that Abraham was on a ship which was bringing British troops to Gallipoli. The ship had to go close to the shore to disembark the troops. In doing this the ship was grounded or went ashore and it was some time before it could be refloated. In the meantime it came under attack from the Turks. In the course of being hit, Abraham was injured and crushed many of his teeth, which caused him to get false teeth later. He and a few other men were on a lifeboat for four or five days before being rescued. He hated to go to the dentist and she thinks it's because of the extent of damage and having to get the false teeth. George and Catherine Dixon of William Street House, Wexford, had four sons, three of whom, Abraham, Edward and George, were at sea at that time. Moya Dixon was married to Capt. Nicholas McGrath who was also at sea at this time and had to abandon ship. *(Mary Corcoran, Dixon family Collection)*

THE Q SHIPS

In December of 1914 the concept of decoy ships or "Q" ships was mooted and to provide the hardware for this scheme the British Admiralty took over some 200 vessels of various types, from trawlers, to barques to tramp steamers. They were armed with 12 pounders, Lewis guns, Depth Charges and various other weapons. All guns etc. were hidden on deck in false packing cases or even in mock-ups of ships lifeboats that would come apart at a touch, leaving the guns ready for action. The intention was to appear helpless to German submarines, who in order to save using torpedoes, would surface to shell and sink the "helpless" ship. Alternately they could board the victim and place charges on her. The plan was simple in theory. As soon as the surfacing submarine fired its warning shot, the "Q" ship sent a "panic party" away in the lifeboats as if abandoning ship, leaving Royal Navy men, concealed around the ship to handle he guns. Then when the U.Boat came in close for the kill, the White Ensign was struck and the guns opened up on the submarine. The Cymric, a three masted sailing vessel, was one of the vessels designated a "Q" ship and was employed in 1918. Whatever her record, she had at least one significant "kill". On 15 October, 1918, she sank, in error, the British submarine H.M.S. J6. At the time of later 1916 and Independence commemorations wits suggested that the surviving crewmen should have been given War of Independence service medals. She was one of the very last sailing ships to enter and leave Wexford port after thousands of years of tradition and consummate skill. During World War Two she sailed literally out of her depth to bring back cargo from neutral Portugal. She crossed the Bay of Biscay en route to Lisbon and disappeared without trace.

The three-masted sailing ship "Cymric" unloading coal at Commercial Quay.

A French naval swivel gun retrieved by trawler skipper Michael Greenwood a little to the south of the Saltee Islands. The swivel gun was operated from a fishing trawler in the desperate battle against the u-boats to preserve trans-atlantic supplies. It had tragic consequences for some trawler crews where it was found that the backfire from the gun capsized the trawler upon which it was bolted. The retrieved gun is on permanent display outside MacCarthaigh's hostelry and restaurant, The Wooden House, at Kilmore Quay. The inscription on the gun reads: St. a C! Mo 1887 N' 686-300 K Pour C.T.R. de 47

A group of Royal Navy sailors from the Wexford coast who survived the debacle created by Winston Churchill when the Allies attempted to land in Turkey. It was in a zone which still lives in memory as the Dardanelles and as a campaign of horrific stupidity. At back, Willie Lambert, Tagoat; Paddy Walsh, Churchtown, Carne. Front, Frank Murphy and his brother Stephen from Ballyhitt.
(Duncannon Fort Maritime Museum Collection)

THE U.S. NAVAL AIRBASE, WEXFORD

The destruction of Allied shipping was so thorough in 1914 and 1915 that the sea around Tuskar Rock was specified as "The Graveyard" – the graveyard of Allied ships. The British Admiralty installed a heavily fortified and top-secret sonar anti-submarine base at The Four Winds, two miles south of Rosslare Harbour overlooking "The Graveyard". It was the earliest of its kind in Europe. A pioneer airman, Major Hugh Clarence Fuller, was ordered by the Admiralty to commission an airship station at Johnstown Castle. It became operational in 1917, but still the U-boats were hunting and sinking. More had to be done as the tide of war hinged precariously.

On 6 April 1917, the United States of America entered the war on the side of the British and French. Major William Sholto Douglas visited Wexford and approved the site proposed by the British War Office for a major seaplane base at Ferrybank inside Wexford Harbour. Towards the end of 1917, the Admiralty had the concrete hangar foundations underway, roads marked off, excavation and drainage completed. However, on the 25th of February, 1918, with no other prospect but that of a long war of attrition, the base was taken over by the United States Navy. As recently uncovered negatives and the Intelligence Chief's diary indicate, it was a development of wide-ranging political and strategic implications. The official U.S. Navy estimation of the base states the case in these words: "The location of this station is most excellent from a strategic point of view, inasmuch as it lies directly at the southern entrance of the Irish Sea, within 12 miles of Tuskar Light. For over four years, Tuskar Rock, one of the most important navigational marks in British waters, has been known as the Graveyard of Ships: many times ships were attacked and sunk by enemy submarines within three or four miles and in plain view from Tuskar Lighthouse. A very considerable amount of allied shipping to and from the United Kingdom had to pass through adjacent waters. As the enemy submarines also used the Irish Sea for a short cut to and from their bases, and it was a fertile field for their operations, the Wexford area was therefore a very busy one for all anti-submarine activity both offensive and defensive. Before the flying boats from this station entered the game, submarines were exceptionally bold within the patrol area of Wexford. The air station is located along the Slaney River across from the City of Wexford; it is well protected from wind, waves and weather due to the almost landlocked harbour. It is also easily accessible to transportation and shipping."

The results of the anti-U-boat operations by the American airmen were immediate. The base became fully operational at the end of September 1918. Within three days of its opening, the "Leinster" was sunk by a U-boat off Dublin. The same submarine was sighted by a Wexford-based seaplane, bombed and crippled in the Irish Sea. Two days later, another U-boat was detected and hit directly, then another, and a fourth. In a brief period the U.S. seaplanes cleared the Tuskar Rock shipping lanes of U-boats.

The total number of U.S. naval personnel was 20 officers and 406 other ranks. To accommodate them, another town had literally been built. It had streets called 42nd St. and 5th Avenue, junctions called Times Square, The Bronx and Brooklyn, a theatre, an orchestra, a hospital, football teams, baseball teams, mighty hangars, row after row of timber houses, and barracks built from nothing in a few months. July 4th was festival day with most of Wexford invited to witness a "World Series" baseball game between the "Cincinatti Bears" and the "Brooklyn Dodgers".

Naval men of many ethnic origins descended on Wexford by launch from their base across the river. Gaiety and mischief was in their hearts, but no echo of malice remains in the folk memory. The economy expanded on all sides.

Security, Espionage.

Security was tight and efficiently unobtrusive. Head of U.S. Intelligence at the base was Chief Petty Officer John J. O'Brien, snr., obviously of Irish descent. The Intelligence Department was not listed in the published crew roll when the base was closed and although the Commanding Officer, Lieut. Commander Victor D. Herbster, commends the Intelligence Department for its excellent weather reports the only place the name John J. O'Brien appears is as a Chief Carpenter's Mate!

O'Brien's diaries contain no classified information but in a lot of weather moans he once, just once, escapes from his trained silence. He notes in annoyance that he has to leave the base to investigate German agents operating in the Rosslare Harbour area. We are left agitated with curiosity for the remainder of the story. Were they German nationals? Michael Collins men? Sympathisers or professionals? Whatever they were, they were in the right place, for the combination of services in the region spearheaded by the U.S. seaplanes had broken the back of the U-boat campaign.

After the failure of Ludendorff's offensive, Germany collapsed. To universal amazement – indeed shock was recorded in the U.S. base – the Great War was suddenly over.

In 1919 when the Americans left for home, the hangars and timber-built quarters and recreation halls were auctioned. They soon formed business premises, large stores and quickly erected buildings all over County Wexford and further afield. Veteran citizens will remember the old Loch Garman Co-Op premises at Trinity Street and Staffords premises on Crescent Quay, Trinity Street and George Murphy's garage and auctioneering premises of Raymond Corish on the Quay. These were formerly hangars and halls from the U.S Naval base. Today, nothing whatever remains of that complex, except the concrete slip opposite Ferrybank Motors from which the great planes rolled like sealions into the water to do battle.

Lt. Commander V. D. Herbster, Commanding Officer Wexford U.S. naval airbase, Ferrybank

Alice White, secretary, U.S. Naval base in Ferrybank, Wexford, 1917-1919, and busy photographer, better known to generations of Wexford's children as the owner of "Alley" White's sweets and ice cream shop at 22 South Main Street, Wexford. She later married Joseph B. Kinsella.

U.S. naval sentries on duty at the entrance to the commanding officer's residence, now Ely House.

Pulling in a seaplane beached at low tide. Whatever the reason the task is being enjoyed.

On standby waiting for the order to take off and the traction to take them down the slip into the water. The concrete slip is all that remains of the U.S. Naval Base today.

Safe landing in Wexford harbour.

Seaplane A 1079

Officers

The "Pioneers", the first to arrive in Wexford to start construction in 1917

The station's American football team.

Radio electricians

The stage in the concert hall, or YMCA hut as it was called, has a colourful backdrop. The Stars and Stripes are over trhe arch while the back drape is made up of the flags of the nations comprising the Allies

The four hangars with two planes and crews.

The U.S. Naval Air Station, Wexford, Ireland, was planned by the British Admiralty early in 1917 but was taken over by the U.S. Navy. The first U.S. Forces to arrive were eight men under Gunner Rogers on 25th February, 1918. Lieut. Comdr. Herbster arrived to take command 28th March, 1918, and from then on things began to hum. Small drafts of men arrived from Queenstown from time to time until there were 232 men and 13 officers on the station 1st July, 1918. By the 1st of August there were 15 officers and 298 men. By the end of October there were 20 officers and 406 men. At no time during the construction period were there sufficient men to build and equip the station as fast as was wished; but, even so, considering the extensive plans and amount of work accomplished, a very remarkable record was made; a record that excelled by far all construction records of Naval Air Stations in Europe. There had been some work done by the British Admiralty before the U.S. forces arrived in Wexford, including the laying of a portion of the foundations for the hangars.

Just before take-off.

Retrieving a wrecked plane.

Under construction 1917.

Over-view of the U.S. base from one of its planes.

The naval base was organized, built and equipped for one purpose — to fight and destroy the German submarines within the area allotted. This was successfully accomplished by the unceasing activities of our forces. After all, it is the hardship surmounted that make up the best part of life. The officers and men can all be proud of everything they have done, for it has been said by those competent to pass judgment that the U.S. Naval Air Station at Wexford has surpassed all other stations in Great Britain, France or Italy, and was the neatest, most up-to-date and best station in Europe.
(Lieut. C. B. Tillotson, Executive Officer)

For a Wexford girlfriend. *(Fintan M. O'Connor Collection)*

Glum looking African-American servicemen at the base. They were described as "Mess Boys". At that time, even in the forces, their gloomy faces were understandable. White "supremacy" was the norm.

High ranking British and U.S. naval personnel with Michael J. O'Connor. The O'Connor family retriever is gripped by their host.
(Fintan M. O'Connor Collection)

A tennis party given by M. J. O'Connor, solicitor (seated centre) and his family for U.S. officers, summer 1918.
(O'Connor Collection)

The ferrybank baseball team competed against other U.S. units stationed within "striking distance" (as they said). The inscription on the shirts reads "U.S. Navy Wexford".

The U.S. naval airbase map showing their planes' radius. An encouraging caption was placed in the left corner.

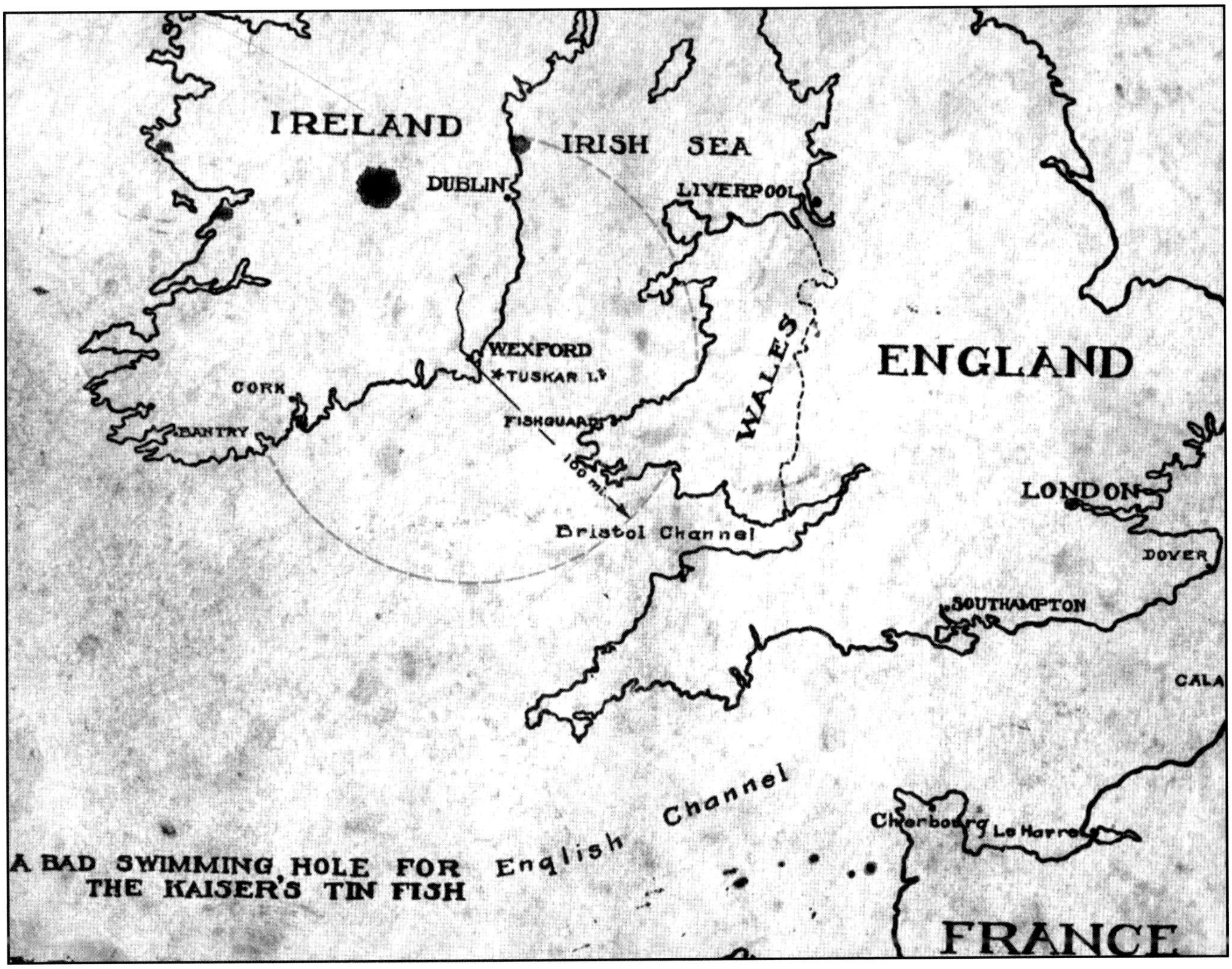

ADMIRAL DAVID BEATTY

Admiral David Beatty of Borodale, Bree, became one of Britain's greatest naval heroes. Born of an Anglo-Irish family the tradition was sport, horsebreeding and hunting. The Admiral's father and grandfather were devoted almost obsessively with horse riding and the County Wexford Hunt. David's grandfather hunted three days a week with two packs of hounds. He was master of the Wexford Hunt for most of his life. The instinct was continued down along the line except with David, born in 1871. An early photo as a child shows him clutching a toy boat. Nevertheless, despite his truly remarkable naval career, he always contrived to synchronise his leave period with the seasons outings of the Wexford Hunt.

Undoubtedly his career of naval triumphs would have rendered him famous. Apart from that it was his "sea-dog bold" appearance, handsome, well-built, trim, cap always at a jaunty angle which made him a publicists ideal, much as Field Marshal Montgomery or Field Marshal Rommel became in World War Two. Postcards with his image in several poses, sketches, paintings in groups, in action or with royalty of several nations, proliferated and were utilised world wide with photogenic success. Not only were his photographs in meetings with British, Belgian and Russian royal heads and leaders widely promoted it is likely that, as far as County Wexford is concerned, his photograph with Tsar Nicholas and the entire tragically ill-fated Russian Royal family is one of the most poignant. Taken during the visit of Beattys battleship, H.M.S. Lion, to Saint Petersburg in 1914.

Beatty proved his competence as a naval commander partaking in such battles as Heligoland Blight, and Dogger Bank. However, his true chance came at the Battle of the Jutland. It was at this battle that he made his famous statement "there appears to be something wrong with our bloody ships today". The Royal Navy's battle cruiser squadron faced heavy losses. However the main part of the Grand Fleet under Jellicoe did not engage the enemy. Both Germany and Britain claimed victory, Britain suffered heavy losses and a "scapegoat" was needed. The admiralty looked towards the difference in loss figures between the Grand Fleet and Beatty's battle cruisers. Jellicoe was criticised for not taking the fleet into action and allowing the German Navy to escape. Jellicoe was desk-appointed First Sea Lord. He was replaced by David Beatty as the Grand Fleet commander.

Amongst the Wexford seamen who served in the British Navy at the Battle of Jutland at least one, Jim Delaney of Wexford, was killed while his brother, Thomas, survived. One of the participants well known to this writer was Matty Berney of rural Clongeen who served as a teenage stoker, not the life on the ocean wave he had anticipated. His presence became known to Beatty. Beatty sought him out and while in calm waters often chatted with him about country life, horses and hunting in Wexford.

Admiral David Beatty.

BEATTY ENTERTAINS THE RUSSIAN IMPERIAL FAMILY

O f all photographs involving Wexford men and women of any spectrum, this photograph of David Beatty entertaining the tragic and ill-fated Russian Imperial family must rank as one of the most dramatic. It was taken by an un-named crew member serving under Rear Admiral Beatty when his battleship, H.M.S. Lion, visited St. Petersburg in summer 1914. This historic photograph found its way to Bonnettstown Hall, County Kilkenny where it remained unseen by anyone except its owner, Commander Geoffrey Marescaux de Saubrit, until September 1982. Seated in front are firstly, left to right, a lady-in-waiting to the Empress; next the Archduchesses Maria, Anastasia, Olga; Lady Buchannon, Grand Duke Cyril's wife is next. The Empress, or as she was known, the Tsarina, holds an umbrella in her hand. Alongside is the Archduchess Tatiana. In the row behind the Archduchess, the officer at left with the gold braided cord on his right shoulder, is Lord Chatfield, Flag Captain to Admiral Beatty. The three young men standing up on chairs were three midshipmen summoned up to entertain the young Archduchesses. The officer, whose face is clearly seen between the two ladies close behind the Tsarina, is Prince George of Batenberg, later the Marquis of Milford Haven, elder brother of Lord Louis Mountbatten. The gentleman in plumed hat and Diplomatic Corps uniform is the British Ambassador to Russia. Next to the British Ambassador is Nicholas, Tsar of All the Russias. At his back with handlebar moustache is Count Fredericks, Grand Marshal of the Imperial Court; alongside the Tsar in his familiar stance is Rear Admiral David Beatty of Borodale, Bree. At the extreme right of the picture is Grand Duke Cyril, who after the assassination of the Imperial family by the Bolsheviks, became Pretender to the Throne of Russia. His son, Grand Duke Vladimir, is the present Pretender and it is interesting to note that it was in that capacity that he attended the funeral of Princess Grace of Monaco.

Another interesting vignette is added to this agreeable scene of terrifying complacency. David Beatty's wife was a very wealthy lady (the daughter of an American multi-millionaire) and she joined him when the naval manoeuvres were finished off St. Petersburg, sailing from London in her own private yacht. She is the lady to the left of the British Ambassador.

Beatty's flagship "Lion" fought in the ferocious naval engagement off Jutland in 1916, said to have been "the only major clash between dreadnought fleets and the last major action in four centuries of naval battles in which guns were the predominant weapon of the sea". Beatty is credited with sinking twelve ships of the Imperial German Navy in that engagement. Beatty's ship "H.M.S. Lion", was the biggest in the British Navy, with a displacement of 26,400 tons. It was 660 ft. long. The beam was 88 ft. and the draught was 27 ft. It was 70,000 horse power and had the fastest speed in the Royal Navy, a maximum of 27 knots. It had eight 13.5 inch guns.

(Photograph by Courtesy of Commander Marescaux de Saubrit)

The young David Beatty of Borodale, Bree, in his sailor suit with toy boat included. For a boy reared in rural County Wexford this proprietary grasp of a favourite toy, a model boat, has plain evidence of his career preferences.

Admiral Beatty inspecting the battle-scarred Liege Fort. Royal Navy, Belgian and British Army personnel accompany him.

Grand Fleet
Commander Jellicoe
replaced by Admiral
Beatty after the Battle
of Jutland.
*(Copy from Cope, Private
Bree donor)*

H.M.S. Lion and inset Admiral Beatty

Fo'esle, H.M.S. Rodney, commanded by
admiral David Beatty.

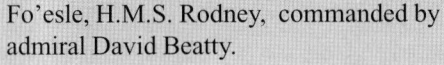

H.M.S. Rodney open to visitors during Navy Week

Admiral Beatty by
Cope. *(Copy by private
donor, Bree)*

H.M.S. Rodney

Admiral David Beatty with King Albert of the Belgians.

Admiral Beatty welcomes
Admiral Benson, U.S.
Navy, on board his
flagship.

One of the best-selling postcard photos of 1919 was taken on Beatty's flagship before the surrender of the German fleet following the sudden collapse of the Central Powers in November 1918. It shows Admiral David Beatty, Admiral Rodham, U.S. Navy; King George the Fifth, Admiral Sims, U.S. Navy and the Prince of Wales who as Edward the Eighth abdicated in 1936.

Major Charles Beatty, brother of Admiral Beatty of Borodale. Charles served in South Africa as ADC to the Brigadier General of the Mounted Infantry Brigade, and during the campaign was twice mentioned in dispatches, awarded the Queen's Medal with six clasps and the DSO. At the outbreak of the First World War he offered his services; in 1916 he was badly wounded at Flanders and had to have an arm amputated. In the summer of that year he returned to his home at Borodale, but was in poor health and died aged 47, in March 1917. He was an accomplished horseman and finished second in the Aintree Grand National of 1897 on Filbert. He also trained the winner of the 1905 Ascot Cup.
(Dan Walsh Collection)

The ruins of Wytschaete captured on 7 June 1917 by the 16th (Southern) Irish and 36th (Ulster) Divisions. Five divisions suffered appalling losses and Major Willie Redmond was mortally wounded.

WESTERN FRONT QUAGMIRE

A late photograph of Major Willie Redmond. He had visibly aged after three years of military and political horror. He was 56 years of age when mortally wounded in the fighting to take Messines Ridge. He was buried at Locre Hospice in Belgium.

Men from the 16th (Irish) and 36th (Ulster) Divisions posed in a
photograph at Major William Redmond's grave.

In September the Mayor of Wexford received £100 from the officers and men of the 36th Division towards the William Redmond memorial fund, and this was given wide publicity. Contributions were received from Carson and many other senior unionists. Major Hutchinson sent £20 raised by all ranks of the 6th Royal Irish Regiment. General Hickie sent £150 raised by officers and men of the 16th Division. The officers of the Tyneside Irish sent £28. The Dublin branch of the memorial fund attracted a particularly distinguished, and politically eclectic membership. Its patron was the Lord Lieutenant, the president was the Lord Chancellor of Ireland. Numbered amongst its vice-presidents were the Church of Ireland Archbishop of Dublin, the Lord Chief Justice of Ireland, Lieutenant General Sir Bryan Mahon, the Earl of Dunraven, and the presidents of University College and the Royal Academy of Medicine.

When a delegation from the memorial committee (Nicholas Byrne, Mayor of Wexford; Myles Keogh, High Sheriff of Dublin; Dr James Ashe, secretary to the committee) visited Willie Redmond's grave in September of that year to plant on it a sod of shamrock from Vinegar Hill, troops from North and South Irish units — an Inniskilling contingent from the 36th Division and Willie Redmond's own Royal Irish Regiment — mounted the guard of honour.

Michael Keogh was living in County Carlow when he decided to join the British Army in World War I. He was made a prisoner by the Germans and later joined Roger Casement's Brigade, recruited from Irish prisoners of war in Germany. Photographed with two comrades, the Shamrock emblem on his lapel was the Brigade's insignia on the German uniform. Had he and his comrades been recaptured or repatriated there is little doubt but that they would have been executed.

Michael Keogh returned safely to Ireland, fought in the War of Independence and following the Treaty he was commissioned in the Free State Army. After the death in action of Michael Collins he left Ireland and returned to Germany.

Officer brothers from different units of the British Army home on leave in Co. Wexford.
(Ann Cogley Collection)

Martin Doyle receives
the Victoria Cross from
Queen Mary

Martin Doyle of New Ross

A handshake from Queen Mary for Company Sergeant Major Martin Doyle of New Ross when he was decorated with the Victoria Cross, Britain's highest award for bravery under fire, by King George V at Buckingham Palace, 8th May 1919. He was born on the 26th October 1891, the only son among six daughters of Larry Doyle and Bridget Fardy, then living at Nash, Gusserane. On St. Stephen's Day 1909, he was enlisted in the British Army. He saw service in India but at the outbreak of war, in 1914, he was returned to Ireland. In December that year, and now serving with the Dublin Fusiliers, he was posted to France. He fought at the Battle of Mons and was one of the lucky ones who survived, for many thousands died in that battle alone. He was promoted Sergeant later in 1915. Rising through the ranks to Company Sergeant Major (CSM), and transferred to the 1st Battalion Munster Fusiliers, he won his first medal for bravery, the Military Medal (MM), on the 24th March 1918, while serving at Hattenfield in France.

Following the war, having survived the gas, the bombs and the bullets, he remained in France on demobilization duties. After a leave period at home, he was summoned to Buckingham Palace to receive his medals on 8th May 1919. He was the only Irishman of the group who received their medals from King George V that day. Returning to New Ross, he was given a hero's welcome by the townspeople.

On 25th November 1919 he married Charlotte Kennedy of New Ross in Westland Row church, Dublin and set up home in New Ross with his new bride. Martin Doyle retired from the British Army in July 1919 and immediately joined the IRA on active service in the War of Independence. The

War of Independence was then at its height and very shortly, in March 1920, the Black and Tans, and later the Auxiliaries, arrived. As an Intelligence Officer in the Mid-Clare Brigade, IRA, Martin Doyle served throughout 1920 and 1921 in Ennis. On one occasion, he was sent to Kilrush on a mission, but due to unreliable information, he almost walked into a trap, "escaping only by the skin of his teeth". When the truce came about in July 1921, he joined the new Free State Army on 20th February 1922, and saw action during the Civil War 1922/23 in Waterford, Kilkenny and South Tipperary. He remained in the National Army at Kilkenny Barracks until he retired in 1937. After securing employment as a security officer with Guinness Brewery in Dublin, he joined the 2nd Battalion Dublin Army Reserve, finally ending his chequered military career in 1939.

Martin Doyle died in Sir Patrick Dun's Hospital, Dublin, on 20th November 1940. He was then living with his family at 23 Larkfield Park, Kimmage. This Wexford soldier of three armies and three wars is buried in

Company Sergeant Major Martin Doyle, March 1918.

Grangegorman military cemetery, near McKee Barracks, Dublin, where his old comrades in the Munster Fusiliers erected a memorial in his honour. According to family legend, when he was only 15 years, though claiming he was 17, he enlisted m the British Army but his father sold a cow to bail him out. He rejoined on St Stephen's Day 1909.

The funeral cortege of John Edward Redmond approaches John Street through Hill Street, Wexford, in March 1918.

Waiting for the arrival of John Edward Redmond's remains at Redmond Square, Wexford, March, 1918. The Redmond monument has been thoroughly draped in black.

The funeral of John Edward Redmond. The cortege progressed around Wexford town before internment in the Redmond vault in St. John's Churchyard, John Street. It is seen here passing through Roches Road by the "Deadery", the main old graveyard, now the site of the Garda Barracks and the site of severe siege warfare in 1169 when King Diarmait MacMurchada and his Norman auxiliaries laid siege to Viking Wexford. *(Sinnott Collection)*

THE WAR OF INDEPENDENCE

The Central Powers of Germany, Austro-Hungary and Turkey unexpectedly collapsed and on 11 November 1918 a cease-fire was declared. The following month a general election throughout Britain and Ireland took place. Sinn Féin won 73 seats out of 105 for the whole of Ireland. They fulfilled their pledge to abstain from the Westminster parliament and they set up a republican parliament, Dáil Éireann. The first Dáil met in the Mansion House, Dublin, on 21 January 1919. They met without the 36 other elected Sinn Féin members who, when their names were called, were declared "Fé ghlas ag gallaimh" – imprisoned by the foreigner.

The Sinn Féin aim was to boycott the established British institutions and system. They asserted the sole power of the Dáil to make laws for the people of Ireland. They demanded 'the evacuation of our country by the English garrison'. Eamon de Valera was elected President and the Dáil proceeded to by-pass every possible aspect of Crown authority, including the legal system. Dáil Eireann instituted its own courts which functioned adequately in the country. The Dáil also organised its own police force.

Co. Wexford returned two Sinn Féin members to Dáil Éireann, Dr James Ryan and Roger Sweetman. They had the support of the Labour leader, Richard Corish. The significance of their electoral victory is that they displaced two very strong and distinguished Redmondite members, Peter Ffrench and Sir Thomas Esmonde.

On the day the first Dáil met, hostilities opened in Soloheadbeg, Co. Tipperary. Soon the entire country saw guerilla war tactics employed against Britain's security forces. The Sinn Féin organisation, its institutions, offices and members along with the Irish Republican Army columns were now at war or in active subversion of the Crown government in Ireland. There was a considerable number, particularly the diminished Redmondites, who disagreed with Sinn Féin policies and activities. Between the two groups a growing bitterness and contempt prospered.

Amongst the Royal Irish Constabulary barracks in Co. Wexford that were attacked, burned or demolished were those of Clonroche, Ferns, Kilmore, Oylegate, Ballinaboola, Tintern, Duncormick, Blackwater, Ballybrazil near Campile, Castlebridge, Ballycanew and Gorey. The RIC then enrolled the first of several thousand English recruits called the 'Black and Tans'. Raids and counter-raids, burning of Sinn Fein members' properties, revenges, ambushes, assassinations and intimidation were persistent occurrences.

The British Post Office became a target and branches throughout County Wexford were put out of commission by a variety of methods including burning. In a famed instance the son of the local postmaster, an active service IRA volunteer, was one to break down a new door to gain entry. His father indignantly protested. "If I thought you were going to smash the good new door I would have let you in from the back." The ensuing two years of guerilla warfare caught world attention, particularly in the U.S.

WEXFORD INSULTED

Read what Father O'Flanagan has said ot Wexford's noblest son :—

"I would be sorry when John Dillon died that it would be necessary for his friends to steal his body down the backways and lanes to Ballaghadereen **to prevent an outraged people from throwing it into the Liffey, as was the case with John Redmond.**" — Father O'Flanagan in a speech opposite Mr. John Dillon's residence in Ballaghadereen, November 17.

Are you going to tolerate this insult to the dead ?

Can we expect anything better from the man to whom the Very Rev. J. O'Callaghan, P.P., Rathdrum, referred to in his sermon on Sunday, October 20th ?

Taking as his text the words—" Render unto Cæsar the things that are Cæsar's, and to God the things that are God's," he emphasised the necessity for obedience to the Church and to God. He went on to say that the newspapers yesterday proclaimed that numbers of Catholics went to listen to a suspended priest addressing them. Those who did it, whether in ignorance or not, would have to answer to God for it. They dishonoured the authority of His Church. What authority could they honour after that ? Not their own. Let them repent and ask God to forgive them, and to open their eyes to see what they had done.

Can you support a policy which acknowledges such a man as one of its chief exponents, and which includes abstention from the House of Commons, so emphatically condemned by our own Bishop as an unwise policy ?

Whose advice are you going to follow—our worthy Bishop's or that of a suspended priest ?

Electors of Wexford, Uphold the Honour of the Model County and avenge the insult to our dead.

VOTE for FFRENCH.

UP REDMOND, and GOD SAVE IRELAND !

Printed and Published by W. M. Corcoran, at "The Free Press" Offices, 59, South Main Street, Wexford.

WHY DID THEY DIE?

BRIAN BORU	1014	**NOT**	to give a colourable sanction to the slavery of Ireland.
EARL OF DESMOND	1467		
SHANE O'NEILL	1567		
HUGH ROE O'DONNELL	1605		
OWEN ROE	1649	**NOT**	to secure the Partition of Ireland.
BISHOP McMAHON	1650		
FATHER SHEEHY	1766		
ARCHBISHOP O'HURLEY	1798	**NOT**	to pledge to a foreign Government the treasure and the manhood of Ireland.
FR. JOHN MURPHY	1798		
LORD EDWARD FITZGERALD	1788		
WOLFE TONE	1798		
EMMET	1803		
O'NEILL CROWLEY	1867	**NOT**	to enable out-of-date political hacks to bargain over Ireland.
PEARSE	1916		
CONNOLLY	1916		
ASHE	1917		
COLEMAN	1918		

THEY DIED TO SECURE THE LIBERATION OF THE OLDEST POLITICAL PRISONER IN THE WORLD—

IRELAND!

RELEASE THE PRISONERS!

RELEASE IRELAND!

Peter Ffrench, M.P., Nationalist Party, Westminster, at his home, Harpoonstown House, Mulrankin, with his second wife, widow of Walter Kehoe, formerly Elizabeth Power of Ballinahask. He lost his seat to Dr. James Ryan in the Sinn Féin electoral avalanche of 1918.

The August 1918 Sinn Féin election land-slide. Myles Redmond of Wexford, a prisoner in Cork Jail, gets a telegraph signed "Doyle" telling of Dr. James Ryan's electoral victory in the home constituency. It states "Ryan wins by 518"

Comrades, pall-bearers, Fianna Éireann scouts surround the coffin of Commandant Séamus Rafter of Monalee, Ballindaggin. He was killed in a munitions explosion at his Enniscorthy home on August 12, 1918. From left, Michael O'Connor, Michael Davis, Denis O'Brien, Patrick Keegan, Loftus Smith, T. D. Sinnott, Fr. Walsh, Albert Smith, James Cullen, Patrick Tyrrell, James O'Brien, Patrick Pierce, Seán Moran, Thomas Doyle, unidentified and Michael Smith.

1918 General Election candidate, Commandant Eamon de Valera in Volunteer uniform.

Commandant Séamus Rafter.

Michael Collins, Director of Intelligence, G.H.Q. Staff.

Field Marshal Sir Henry Wilson, Chief of the Imperial General Staff, a determined adversary of the Irish and any form of Irish independence from 1912 onwards. He became a militant adviser to the anti-nationalist administration in Belfast. So virulent was his influence and antagonism that his assassination was ordered and carried out in London on 22 June, 1922.

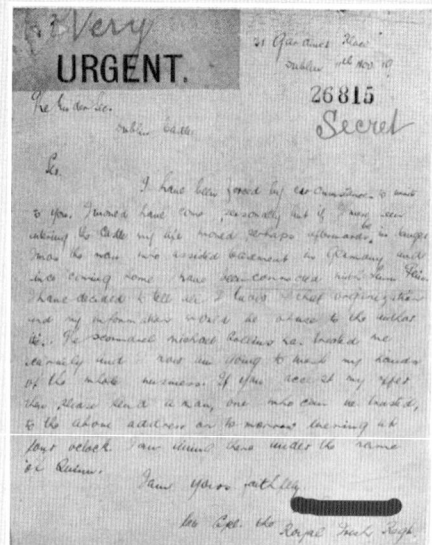

Dublin Castle had been infiltrated at the highest administrative level by Michael Collins' agents. Accordingly this letter to the Under-Secretary of State was passed on to Collins. The writer was from Wexford and was promptly executed on Collins' orders at the place, time and date, the informer arranged himself.

Very Urgent

21 Gardiner Place

Dublin 11 Nov. 19 (No year)
The Under Secretary,
Dublin Castle,
Sir,
I have been forced by circumstances to write to you. I would have come personally but if I were seen entering the Castle my life would perhaps afterwards be in danger. I was the man who assisted Casement in Germany and since coming home have been connected with Sinn Fein. I have decided to tell all I know of that organisation and my information would be of use to the authorities. The scoundrel Michael Collins has treated me scurvily and I now am going to wash my hands of the whole business. If you accept my offer then please send back a man, one who can be trusted, to the above address on tomorrow evening at four o'clock. I am living there under the name of . . . . .
I am yours faithfully

. . . .
Late Corporal, the Royal Irish Regiment.

Hunger strike group 1920. Released from Mountjoy Prison, May 6th 1920, after ten days' hunger strike. Photo taken in the grounds of the Mater Hospital, Dublin, after six weeks treatment. Left to right, front row: P. Byrne, Killannne; Tom Donovan, Killinaule, Co. Tipperary; M. Whelan, Irish St., Enniscorthy. Second row: P. Dalton, Waterford; McMahon, D. Jones, Cork; Higgins. Back row: Leo McKenna, E. Dwyer, Limerick; M. Daveran, Tipperary; J. Coughlan, Cork.

Taken in Wexford town during the war of Independence. There is no explanation. The decorators could be British soldiers or the IRA. It was a tactic used by both sides.

(Michael J. O'Connor Collection)

One of the British Army armoured steam engines of the Dublin South Eastern Railway line. Two heads, probably the driver and stoker, peer out at the cameraman. *(Sinnott Collection)*

British armoured train, Dublin Rosslare Harbour line, 1920-21. The "Tommies" slogan is incomplete. The guns protruding from the slits are water-cooled Vickers machine guns. *(Sinnott Collection)*

NED FOLEY'S SHOP BURNED

One of the Sinn Féin family businesses targeted by the military was Edward Foley's of North Main Street Wexford, opposite Hassett's the chemists (Foley's later transferred to Crossabeg). The late James Kelly N.T. (Kelly's bakery family) gave us this description in 1986:

"One other event on the Main Street in those years should not be forgotten, and that was the burning of Ned Foley's, 14 North Main Street, in the summer of 1920. There was curfew then and people had to be off the streets at nine. My father drove us home in the pony and trap after a visit to relatives in the country, and at 8.30 p.m., when we got to Rowe Street, the block was sealed off by the R.I.C. and Black and Tans as far as Anne Street. We were allowed through because we lived there, but in the middle of the night, we children were wakened and carried out on to the street in blankets. I still remember vividly the flames licking across the street at Mrs. Mylie Doyle's stationery shop (Hassett's), which was badly damaged. We were brought up to Lar Kelly's house on Waterloo Road and put to bed there. He was then Manager of the Home and Colonial Stores, beside the Mechanics Institute, where Harry and Willy Stone served their time. No. 16, John F. Kehoe's drapery shop, over which the Tierney family lived (Mr. Tierney was Manager of Tylers — Bargain Stores) was also burned to the ground.

No. 18 was next and the firemen brought a hose through the shop door, upstairs and out through the back bedroom window. It was leaking and had to be covered with empty sacks in many places. My mother put a statue of St. Anthony out through the same window."

Michael Parker and Edward Foley, both Wexford shopkeepers and Sinn Féin members.
(Shane Sinnott Collection)

Joe Anderson of Coolmeelagh, Bunclody, who as a member of the North Wexford Brigade, ran dispatches for Collins and acted as his bodyguard

Sinn Féin family. A typical situation in many families arose during the War of Independence. In this photograph of the Williams family, taken at their home in the parish of Taghmon, at least three were on active service apart from political support. Standing: May, a member of Cumann na mBan, imprisoned in England when found carrying information for the IRA; Annie, Frances, Thomas, who was jailed three times for his republican roles between 1918 and 1923; Kathleen, Lillie, Gretta whose activities in the cause compelled her to emigrate. Seated: Jack, Mrs Kate Williams and her husband, Laurence, with their youngest daughter Helena. *(Tomás Williams collection)*

Black and Tans take a suspect into custody. *(Sinnott Collection)*

The home of the Doyle Brothers at Auburn Terrace, Wexford.

MARTIAL LAW

The proclamation of martial law displayed on the window of the Doyle family home in Auburn Terrace, Wexford. Above it, in destruction inviting defiance, is the Irish tricolour. The Doyle brothers, owners of the Selskar Iron Works (modern Dunnes Stores), had refused orders for British war production in 1914. They later sheltered Irish volunteers "on the run". In addition they manufactured guns, bullets and hand grenade casings in their foundry. Several times their home and premises were destined to be burned by Crown forces but they were always given discreet hints by Sergeant Collopy of the R.I.C. None of the family was injured. The family slept, for some time, with their clothes at the end of their beds for quick dressing. They moved their machinery to a rural base and continued to manufacture bullets and arms for the I.R.A. Alderman William Doyle, J.P., friend of Arthur Griffith, was an early Sinn Féin supporter. He was a Gaelic Leaguer and later was appointed a Judge of the Sinn Féin Courts in active opposition to the Crown Courts. Their home was frequently raided and ransacked by the military. The display of the martial law proclamation in their parlour window was maintained under threat of death. But the tricolour was maintained over it as long as it remained there. Hundreds of Wexford people took walks to Auburn Terrace to see the tableau themselves. Every morning, Captain Parkes, an army officer who had a wooden arm with a hook for a hand, rode past the house to check if the proclamation was still in the window.

Tom Cousins (second from left) with a group of workmates in Drinagh Cement Works. He became a noted War of Independence and Civil War veteran. He was a Captain in the Irish Free State army and also entered local politics.
(Maggie Cousins collection)

Members of the North Wexford Battalion, IRA. Back row: left to right: Thomas Dugdale, James Keys, Peter Kenny, William Redmond, Michael Keys. Middle row: Martin Reville, Thomas Stafford, Michael Reddy, Joseph O'Toole. Front row: Myles Kenny, Philip Purcell, Denis Kavanagh, Edward Poundall.
(Michael Fitzpatrick Collection).

A brief account by Seán Sinnott of Dempsey's Terrace, Wexford, on the founding of Sinn Féin in Wexford and his subsequent role.

Gearr Chuntas a scríobh Seán Sionóid a d'eag 1970.

MY ACTIVITIES IN THE NATIONAL STRUGGLE

Joined Sinn Féin in 1904; attended the first Convention of Sinn Féin in the Rotunda in 1905. E. Martin of Tulla presided. Sworn into the I.R.B. by Seán T. O'Kelly in 1906. Worked in Sinn Féin till the start of the Volunteers in 1913. Took part in the general mobilisation for Easter Sunday which was cancelled. During the following week tried to mobilise up to the Friday before the surrender but could do nothing here. Tried to organise a few others but as the town was full of military, special constables, and all roads and bridges were held towards Enniscorthy nothing could be done.

Was arrested on June 2nd and sent to the Military Barracks and Waterford Jail. The following Saturday sent to Richmond Barracks, Dublin and a week after conveyed to Stafford Prison and to Frongoch after two months in Stafford. Released in October. In November myself and Robert Brennan were arrested and brought to Cork Jail where I met Sean McCurtin, Terrence McSweeny and George Clancy. Two were murdered and Terrence died on hunger strike. We started on hunger strike and were released on the Cat and Mouse Act after 4 days. I was brought to Terence McSweenys house and after four days in bed returned home. Continued in the Volunteers and took part in Ryan's election in 1918, and continued in the Volunteers until 1920. Carried out a big raid on the Old Distillery (Pierces) and took 500 16lb shell cases.

I was ordered to sleep out and after 3 weeks was arrested and brought to Waterford Jail and Cork Military Detention Barracks. Transferred to Cork Jail and Monday after Bloody Sunday ten of us were sent by a destroyer to Pembroke docks and to Wormwood Scrubs prison. Went on hunger strike there and after a week sent to Brixton Prison. Released from there nine months after.

At that time only a small number of men were left here. I had a meeting in the old Gaelic Hall – myself, F. Carty, James Hayes and some others I forget. We decided to burn some military lorries at the South Station. The next night I went home about 11.30 and was not long in when the house was surrounded again and I was brought to Waterford and from there after a few weeks I was brought to Kilworth Camp and was transferred to Spike Island. Took part in the break up and was sent to Port Laoise (Maryborough). I was released with all the other prisoners after the signing of the Treaty in 1921. I took no part in the Civil War.

Seán.

Seán Sinnott

Men of the Royal Irish
Constabulary in
Enniscorthy
Barracks, Abbey Square,
1920. A P. A. Crane
photograph.
(Garda Síochána Archives)

Veney's residence, North Parade, Gorey,
demolished by the British Army. The Veneys were
outspoken Irish Irelanders.
(Michael Fitzpatrick Collection)

Lea-Wilson Execution

Percival Lea-Wilson D.I. RIC, shot at Gorey 15th June 1920.
(Michael Fitzpatrick Collection)

Percy Lea-Wilson was an English graduate of Oxford University who joined the Royal Irish Constabulary. He served in Dublin during and after the 1916 Rising. Following the surrender in Dublin he was in charge of Irish Volunteer prisoners who were being held overnight in the open air. It was seen that he, particularly, ill-treated prisoners but paid humiliating and public attention to the elderly Fenian and signatory to the 1916 Proclamation, Thomas Clarke. He was offensive, taken note of, and never overlooked. During the War of Independence Lea-Wilson was posted to Co. Wexford as District Inspector, R.I.C., stationed in Gorey. He lived at Westmount. His execution was ordered and he was shot dead outside his residence in June, 1920.

Arrival of the flag draped coffin of District Inspector Lea-Wilson at Christ Church, Gorey.
(Michael Fitzpatrick Collection)

The cortege of District Inspector Lea-Wilson is preceeded by high ranking R.I.C. officers and British military with arms reversed.
(Michael Fitzpatrick Collection)

The Union Jack draped coffin of Inspector Lea-Wilson proceeds with R.I.C. guard of honour followed immediately by his wife, Dr. Marie Lea-Wilson and dignitaries. It is of poignant interest that the recently identified Carravagio painting "The Taking of Christ" came into the possession of the Jesuit Fathers in Dublin from Dr. Lea-Wilson. She was a devout Catholic and a personal friend of the Archbishop of Dublin.

(Michael Fitzpatrick Collection)

Twenty-one members of the armed R.I.C. in Gorey around 1920. Wives and children resident in the barracks are included. *(Michael Fitzpatrick Collection)*

1921: James Davis, Master of Hounds, Killinick Harriers, being handed a written order not to hunt on a particular occasion by an officer of the South Wexford Brigade, IRA.
(Courtesy of Alice Mernagh)

I.R.A. prisoners photographed by a prisoner in Mountjoy Jail, June 1920. The box camera prisoner was John Kavanagh, Clologue, Ferns. The only positive identities we can make are Patrick J. Jordan, Ballindaggin, seated in the centre of the front row. Behind him in vest is Matt Kavanagh, Arklow.
(Courtesy of Patrick J. Jordan)

Active Wexford Presence. The Rathmines Sinn Féin Committee 1918-1919. Standing: Tom O'Connor, Bob Brennan, Wexford and Echo Newspaper; William Sears, Joseph McDonough, George Daly, Thomas Cullen, Séamus Dwyer, Patrick J. Little, George Irwin and Seán Doyle. Seated: Mrs Richard Mulcahy (nee Ryan, Tomcoole), Mrs Kent, Mrs French-Mullen and Dr. Kathleen Lynn. P. J. Little, T.D. for Waterford was later Minister for Posts and Telegraphs in the de Valera government and was of particular benefit to the Wexford Opera Festival in the early fifties. He was a grand-uncle of Ian Hearne, former head of the Wexford Engineering Co. (Star Iron Works).

A County Wexford contingent at the Irish Language Summer School in the Ring Gaelteacht, Co. Waterford, July 1918
(Kathleen Browne Collection)

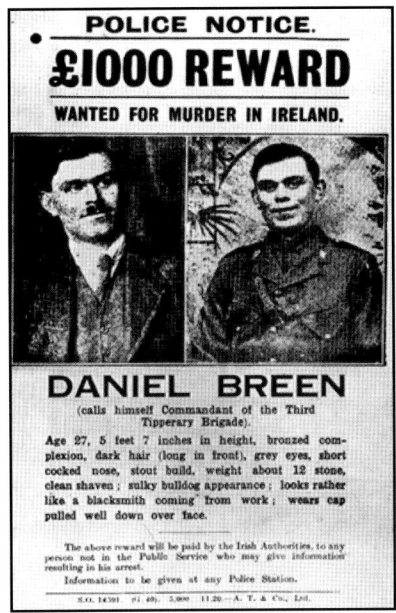

The wedding of the active Tipperary revolutionary, Dan Breen, took place at the height of the War of Independence when there was a price of 1,000 pounds sterling on his head. He married Brighid Malone on 12 June 1921 under heavy IRA security. The wedding photo tells its own story. The bridesmaid was Áine Malone. His bestman was his close comrade in arms, Seán Hogan. The wedding took place at Glenagat House, the residence of Michael Purcell and family between Clonmel and Cahir town, both garrisoned. The officiating priest was the Franciscan, Fr. Ferdinand O'Leary of Wexford town.

WAR WEDDINGS

War weddings take place in times of extreme of stress no matter how happy the day or contented the smiles. In World War One soldiers and the girls they loved usually married on leave and in the knowledge that the groom might be killed on return to battle.

Weddings of active participants in Irelands War of Independence had an added anxiety. Usually the groom was a wanted man. Not only that but many of the guests, men and women, were wanted by the British authorities as well. This is well illustrated in the marriage group photograph taken at the 1918 wedding of Sean T. O'Ceallaigh to Mary Kate Ryan of Tomcoole, Taghmon. By tradition this would have taken place in much raided Tomcoole but it took place in Rathmines, Dublin. Had the military raided this leafy garden with moderate success they would have arrested about twenty of the most influential pillars of the Sinn Fein movement and many more of the guests who had already served terms in prison or had been sentenced to death.

Clergy and some guests: Fr. Ferdinand O'Leary, O.F.M., who officiated at the wedding of Dan Breen. Also in the photo are Fr. Frank Davin, Jerome Davin, the bridegroom Dan Breen and Seán Cooney. Fr. Fedinand from Carrigeen, Wexford, was uncle of Liam Devereux, Mrs. Ena Quirke and Mrs Betty Harpur, formerly of Carrigeen, Wexford.

Fr. Ferdinand O'Leary O.F.M., Carrrigeen, Wexford, a native of the Carrigeen-Grogans Road Sinn Féin "Triangle".

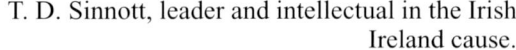

T. D. Sinnott, leader and intellectual in the Irish Ireland cause.

The wedding of Seán T. O'Ceallaigh to Mary Kate Ryan of Tomcoole, Taghmon in Rathmines Church, Dublin, took place on Easter Monday 1918. The reception was held at 19, Ranelagh Road, Dublin and included as guests a microcosm of the national movement in Ireland before the re-opening of hostilities. Seating on the ground are: Jack Ryan, Michael Kelly, brother of Seán T.; Máirín Cregan (Mrs. Jim Ryan), Phyllis Ryan, Chris O'Malley, nee Ryan; Mrs Arthur Conway and Louis. Seated, first row: Fr. Mark O'Byrne, C.C., Wexford; Seán T's mother, Mrs Elizabeth Ryan, the bride's mother; Laurence O'Neill, Lord Mayor of Dublin; Min Ryan (Mrs. Richard Mulcahy); the bride, Mary Kate Ryan; the bestman, Liam O'Briain; John Ryan, father of the bride; Mrs Larry O'Neill, Arthur Conway and Dr. Jim Ryan. Second row: Arthur Cleary, James McCormack, the Wexford chemist, an IRB activist who was involved in the gun running; George Gavan Duffy, unidentified, Fr. Devine; Monsignor Curran, Marion O'Malley, Fr. Martin Ryan, brother of the bride; the groom, Sean T. O'Ceallaigh, later President of Ireland; Denis McCollough, IRB Belfast (married to Agnes Ryan); Mrs Tom Clarke widow of the executed 1916 leader; Mrs Cathal Brugha, Cathal Brugha, Mrs Séamus O'Kelly, Seamus O'Kelly (the writer "Sceilg"), Dick Foley and Liam T. Cosgrave. Third row: Bob Brennan, Tomás O'Máille, Pádraig Kehoe, Glencarrag; Agnes O'Farrelly, Michael O'Maille (married to Chris Ryan); Nellie Ryan, sister; Seán O'Dea, Elizabeth Ryan (sister); Peig Grogan, Ms. Byrne, Margaret O'Kelly (sister of the groom); Mrs Wyse Power, Mrs Coyle, Mrs Dick Foley. Back row: Dr. P. Grogan, Ballymore Eustace; Mattie Kelly, Mrs George Gavan Duffy, Dora French, Fr. Pádraig de Brún, mathematician and poet; Fr. Michael Murphy, C.C. Taghmon, a very colourful supporter of the Gaelic League and Sinn Féin; Fr. Paul Walsh, historian; unidentfied, Seán McGarry, Kathleen Browne, Rathronan Castle; two unidentifieds and Michael Ryan, the bride's brother.

Wedding of Pádraig Kehoe and Josephine Hayes

One of the most inspirational leaders of the Irish Ireland movement and Sinn Féin, farmer, poet, writer, orator, Pádraig Kehoe of Glencarrig, Enniscorthy, married Josephine Hayes of Enniscorthy in the very year that the War of Independence broke out, 1919. As well as the clergy from their parishes, the guests included the most influential Sinn Féin activists in County Wexford while the most distinguished guest of national significance was the founder of Sinn Féin, Arthur Griffith. Sean T. O'Ceallaigh later President of Ireland, is believed to have been present but is not in the photo. We have been unable to identify some of the guests at the time of writing but we are very grateful to a daughter of the bride and groom, Nurse Kitty Kehoe, for her help. Her brother Padge, winner of three All-Ireland hurling medals and two National Hurling League medals in the 1950s and 60s, is probably the most famous of the family today. Front row: Thomas D. Sinnott, later County Manager; A. N. Other, Stephen Hayes, Alice Byrne, Peter Hayes, Nellie Hayes, Tommy Hayes, A. N. Other, A. N. Other, Michael O'Hanlon, later Senator. Second row: Fr. Browne, St. Aidan's Cathedral; A. N. Other, the bride's mother, Ellen Hayes; Annie Hayes; Fr. Patrick Murphy, House of Missions. Below him seated is the bride, Josephine Hayes, and next to her the groom, Pádraig, later Senator. Next are: Joseph Sinnott, Katie Keating, father of the bride; Thomas Hayes, Fr. John Codd, later Monsignor, Archdeacon and Dean of the Diocese while P.P. Ferns; Seamus O'Dubhghaill, who had been Brigade Adjutant of the Irish Volunteers in 1916; A. N. Other and Fr. Patrick Cummins, St. Aidan's Cathedral, an irrepressible Gaelic League promoter. In the back row there is John Hayes, John Barker, on whose premises in South Main Street, Wexford, new recruits to the Irish Republican Brotherhood were sworn in by Seán T. O'Ceallaigh; P. D. Breen, N.T., sportsman and later President of the G.A.A; underneath him, George Hayes. Next is Philip Hayes and John Sinnott of Garrywilliam House, Crossabeg. Second from right at John Sinnott's right is his sister, Mary Sinnott.

Wedding of
General Tom Barry

The wedding of General Tom Barry in Vaughan's Hotel, 22 August, 1921. Amongst the guests, sitting in front, 4th from left, are Mrs. Richard Mulcahy, nee "Min" Ryan, Tomcoole and Gearóid O'Sullivan. Seated, 2nd from left, Harry Boland; sixth from left Liam Deasy, the Bride, Leslie Price; Eamon de Valera, Tom Barry. At extreme right, seated from right, Countess Marcievicz and Mary MacSweeney, sister of Terence, Lord Mayor of Cork who died on hunger strike. First row, standing at extreme left, Seán Lehane, 5th from left Jim Hurley, Ted Sulivan and Michael Collins who, wary of personal security, bends his head; 10th from left, Richard Mulcahy; 12th from left Eoin O'Duffy, 16th from left, Emmet Dalton, 20th from left, Rory O'Connor. Last row, 2nd from left, Seán Hales; Liam Devlin and far right, Joe O'Reilly. The developments following the Treaty with Britain devasted those in this happy truce period wedding photograph. The division which developed murderously saw the Mulcahy, Michael Collins, Gearoid O'Sullivan, Seán Hales, Eoin O'Duffy, Emmet Dalton and Joe O'Reilly take the pro-treaty side.

Eamon de Valera, Tom Barry, Rory O'Connor, Harry Boland, Liam Deasy, Countess Marcievicz and Mary MacSweeney took the anti-treaty side. Jim Hurley, 3rd to the left of Michael Collins was a member of the ambush party at Béal na mBláth in which Collins was killed. *(Ryan Collection).*

Peadar Sinnott in the wars but in safe hands. Snapshot taken during the War of Independence but the location is not stated.
(Sinnott Collection)

1920: Another cultural leap forward with the foundation of the Ui Chennselaig Society, the first County Wexford History Society to focus exclusively on its own heritage. Taken at St. Aidan's Presbytery, Enniscorthy. Back, from left: Rev. Patrick Cummins, C.C., Enniscorthy; V. Rev. Robert Fitzhenry, P.P., Our Lady's Island; V. Rev. Thomas O'Byrne, P.P., Piercestown. Front, from left: Rev. Richard Browne, C.C., Enniscorthy; unidentified; V. Rev. John Canon Dunne, P.P., Castlebridge; Kathleen Browne, Rathronan Castle; Professor R. A. S. MacAlister, Litt.D., F.S.A.; W. H. Grattan Flood, Mus.D., K.S.G.; unidentified; V. Rev. Mark O'Byrne, P.P., Ballindaggin.

Throughout the War of Independence the Labour Party allied itself with Sinn Féin. This photograph of Wexford Corporation Labour members was taken by Charles Vize in 1920. Though impossible to visualise at the time, Wexford's first Labour Mayor, the outstanding orator, politician and Labour veteran, Alderman Richard Corish, was to be re-elected Mayor yearly until his death in 1945. Front row: Councillors Thomas O'Brien, Bride Street; Jack Walsh, Bride Street; Alderman Richard Corish, Mayor; Councillors Thomas Rossiter, Dempsey's Terrace; Joseph Boyce, Abbey Street. Back row: Councillors James Crosbie, Roche's Terrace; James Sinnott, The Faythe; a Dublin Trade Union Organiser; Mr. John Kehoe, Town Sergeant; Alderman James Larkin, High Street; Councillors Michael Martin, The Faythe; David O'Neill, Thomas Street.

"Pax" Sinnott during active service with the North Tipperary Brigade I.R.A., 1921. Peadar Sinnott was one of eleven children born into a strongly nationalist family in Newtown, Ballygarrett. He chose medicine as a career and in later life became one of the most famous doctors in general practice at Rocklands, Wexford. For many years he was a member of the Irish International Clay Pigeon shooting team, a founder member of the Wexford Historical Society and himself a competent local historian. *(Sinnott Collection)*

In this period the medical student, Peadar Sinnott, made and tested a home-made explosive for use by I.R.A. units in the field. To identify its unique qualities he called it "Paxo" indicating that peace was ultimately the desired outcome. This gave rise to the name by which he was known for the remainder of his life, "Pax". He died unexpectedly in March 1957.

We are not publishing his recipe, a recipe which enjoyed success – if that's the appropriate phrase – but indicate some of the hazards involved in home manufacture by quoting his final instruction: "Care should be taken that the pans used should not be chipped and they must not be used without hot plate. They must be wiped on the outside after each operation."

"Pax" Sinnott on active service in the North Tipperary Brigade area, I.R.A., 1921

(Sinnott Collection)

SINN FÉIN COURT

Former IRA chief-of-staff, Seán McBride

The Sinn Féin Court sitting in Castlebar, Co. Mayo, shows the accepted arrangements. Before a case was opened a form of agreement accepting arbitration was signed by the parties involved. Two of the IRA police are identified standing, caps on, in stand-at-ease position. By the spring of 1920 Sinn Féin courts were functioning smoothly. The courts enjoyed considerable success, especially with land and farm disputes. The "agitators" were invited to bring their claims before the Dáil Éireann or Sinn Féin courts rather than to the "enemy courts". In that way the Sinn Féin courts often brought about agreement between landlords and tenants, between proprietors and landless families. They began to take over some of the criminal business. Chief Justice Conor Maguire later commented, "It was quite amazing that Dublin Castle ignored our activities for so long."

In our photograph the Claremorris solicitor, Mr. Conor Maguire, at centre behind table, presided. He later became Attorney-General in 1932, judge of the High Court 1936, Chief Justice 1946, decorated by the French and German governments, member of the Commission for Human Rights under the Council of Europe 1962. He was married to Miss Norah Whelan, Drinagh House, Wexford. They have three sons, Judge Conor Maguire, later Head, European Union Bureau, Dublin; Dr. Brian Maguire, Athy, and our photo donor, Peter Maguire, Senior Counsel, Ballymore, Killinick, County Wexford.

In February, 1977, Seán McBride, the former United Nations High Commissioner in Namibia, visited Rosslare Harbour. He stayed at the Harbour View Hotel where 55 years previously along with Mr. de Valera and Mr. Séan Noonan, all three "on the run", had a meal before slipping through a police and army net to escape from the country.

Mr. McBride recalled: "Mr de Valera was disguised as a priest. I was his secretary, With Mr. Noonan, who subsequently became Irish Ambassador in Washington, we wanted to get to Paris to attend an Irish Race Conference there." The conference took place on 22nd January 1922.

"We knew that the Dublin-Rosslare boat train was under close surveillance so we got Tony Woods to drive us by car from Dublin to Rosslare Harbour. At the time what is now the Harbour View Hotel was a boarding house. I remember we had tea and boiled eggs on arrival."

"We dared not approach the pier until the boat express train arrived from Cork. Then we split up. We mingled with the train passengers, walked boldly up the gangway and boarded the ship under the very eyes of the police and military." *(Photograph by courtesy of Hotel Rosslare)*

General Richard Mulcahy in new Irish Army uniform photographed with his wife "Min" Mary Josephine nee Ryan of Tomcoole at their home, Lissenfield, 1922.
(Ryan family Collection)

THE TRUCE

Following two and a half years of guerrilla warfare against the British forces and government, the British Prime Minister sent a letter to President de Valera proposing a conference with a view to peace. The date was 25 June 1921. A truce was declared between the troops under the control of Dáil Éireann and the London government which came into effect on July 9, 1921. This development was, in view of Britain's world power status, perceived as tantamount to outright victory by the the soldiers and officers' units and officials of Dáil Éireann with unconcealed delight and relief. Fighters "on the run", mobile columns, all recently hunted personnel and administrators in city, town and country, came back into the light of day and associated openly without anxiety.

The fighting men returned to their home areas and in that period of understandable euphoria they rested, regrouped, trained, enjoyed recreation and recruited. These citizen soldiers expected that unqualified independence had been won. Naive indeed one can say with the luxury of hindsight. Nevertheless there is a comparison with team sportsmen who at the beginning of a championship would not have peaked but who had the hope and intention of reaching that state. In the summer of 1921 the idea of humiliation or anything less than respect and independence was unthinkable.

For the rest of that summer Irish Republican Army Volunteers came in from the war zones. In County Wexford the secluded and as yet unidentified "safe houses" opened their gates and doors. Those many "safe houses" in County Wexford were in use throughout the War of Independence where Volunteers in danger of capture for a specific operation found shelter. Neither houses nor fugitives were recorded, naturally, but houses like Sinnotts of Dempsey's Terrace or Sinnotts of Newtown, Ballygarret housed "men on the run" from Ulster to the Cork, Tipperary, Connacht and West Munster areas of operations.

For the summer of 1921, however, an unusual phase of alert but contented leisure obtained.

Joseph McKelvey wearing the newly issued Irish army officers uniform in 1922. He took the republican side in the Civil War and was executed along with Rory O'Connor, Liam Mellows and Dick Barrett on December 8, 1922, by the Free State government in reprisal for reprisal attacks. The specific republican attack had been upon T.D's who were Treaty supporters. One of them, Sean Hales, T.D., died. In the saga of revenge and counter revenge the republican attack on December 7 had been to avenge the execution by the Free State of Erskine Childers on 24 November, 1922.

Flying column unit in familiarity training.
There are no names or location quoted in this
photograph from the Shane Sinnott collection.

Rory O'Connor, Chairman, Acting Military Council,
Irish Republican Army 1922. Eamon de Valera's
reliance on him was summed up in these words: "In
Rory O'Connor and his comrades lives the
indominitable soul of Ireland."O'Connor, during his
brief tenure as Director of Operations in England,
believed in bringing the war to the enemy's door. He
sanctioned the burning of warehouses in English
ports such as Liverpool, attacked the homes of
Black and Tans who were engaged in a campaign of
terror in Ireland, and had plans for incendiary
attacks in London, Birmingham, Sheffield and
Newcastle which proved impractical.

Ballyregan House, Killinick, County Wexford. Dr. James H. Anglim, Dispensary doctor in Broadway, with Rory O'Connor at his home in Ballyregan in 1921. Dr. Anglim was a cousin and sometimes "guardian" of Rory O'Connor who was called "Roddy" in the family. Dr. Anglim died on 11 September 1950, aged 84.

Photo taken in the safety of Ballyregan House precincts. Nevertheless, "Dont Take My Photograph!" *(Anglim Collection)*

Rory O'Connor in the garden of Ballyregan House.

Rory O'Connor, George O'Connor and Jack
Yeats (with revolver) at Anglim's of
Ballyregan House during the 1922 Truce.
*(Anglim Collection. The photos were taken by Mrs.
Lily O'Doherty, nee Anglim).*

Rory O'Connor with the binoculars and revolver
bearing comrade, Jack Yeats, who was apparently
acting as umpire in a target practice competition.

Rory O'Connor at target practice. A competition seems to be in progress. *(Anglim Collection)*

Target practice in Anglim's garden.
(Anglim Collection)

Rory O'Connor has his scores marked at Ballyregan.
(Anglim Collection)

Rory O'Connor with the Anglims in the garden of Ballyrankin House. This series of snapshots was taken on May 22, 1922

IRA Volunteer probably dressed and posed as a member of the proto-Irish Army when taking over a British Army barracks in County Wexford, 1922. Uniforms had not yet been issued. On occasion the withdrawing British Army left their heavier weapons with the newly recognised Irish Army. The light machine gun is a Lewis Gun. Designed by an American of that name and in service with the British army from 1915 to 1939 and with the Irish Army from 1922 to c.1948. It had an aluminium barrel casing, which was designed to draw air over internal cooling vanes to cool the barrel. Point 303 calibre, weighed 26 lbs. and had a rate of fire of 550 rounds per minute from drum magazine. Gas operated.

"Dancing at the Crossroads" at Anglim's of Ballyregan during the Truce. *(Anglim Collection)*

Fourteen-years-old Peter Donnelly, Green Street, Wexford, Fianna Éireann Scout, 1921. *(Courtesy Donnelly family Collection)*

Commandant J. J. Brennan-Whitmore of Gorey in the newly issued army uniform, pictured with an unidentified cleric. Brennan-Whitmore, a veteran of the Boer War fighting on the side of the British, was a persistent advocate of guerrilla warfare. He thoroughly disagreed with the 1916 strategy of a gesture-like last stand, despite its overwhelming political success.

The South Wexford Brigade, Irish Republican Army, at their training camp in the lands of Ballytory Castle in November 1921.

The photograph was posed outside Ballytory Castle, now the residence of Mr. Chris Doyle. Holding the green, white and orange banner in strange juxta-position of colours at the back is the area's postman, Ned Doyle. Back row, left to right: Jim Browne of Ballycushlane; Jack Stafford, Tacumshane; Tom Delaney, Faythe, Tacumshane; Paddy Kehoe. Bennettstown, a former All-Ireland ploughing champion; Tommy Pettit of Ballyduskar, Killinick; Jack Browne, Carne; Peter Reville, Broadway; Phil Wall, Ballyfane; Paddy Sinnott, Butlerstown, an Irish high jump champion; Robbie Sinnott, Bunarge; Mike Sinnott, Sigginstown; Jack Reville, Broadway, later a Garda Sergeant and champion cyclist.

Second row from back: Jack Murphy; John Fowler, Mayglass; Tom O'Brien, Allenstown; Jim Kehoe, Bennettstown; Bill Hayes, Ballyfane; Aidan Sinnott, Sigginstown; Peter Corish, Ringsheerane, Carne; Ned Sinnott; Bill Doyle, The Chour; Jimmy Byrne of Broadway; Willie Pierce, The Bayteen, Ballytory; John Keane and Pat Keating of Yoletown. Though one of the most unobtrusive of men, quiet and gentlemanly, Pat Keating was regarded as one of the most effective and reliable soldiers in the South Wexford Brigade.

Third row from back: Paddy Parle, Tucumshane; Mike Gaul, Bennettstown; Nick Devereux, The Trap; Tommy Doyle, The Chour; Paddy Cullen, Lady's Island; Paddy Wall, Ballyfane; Phil Furlong, Loughtown; Jack Devereux, Grange, Captain of the battalion; Jim Gaul, Benistown; Jim Devereux, The Trap; Paddy Corry, Ballyfane; Tommy Marley, Broadway; Jim Pettit, Ballycushlane.

Front row: Martin Chambers, Assaly, Killinick; Jack Marley, Kisha; Joe Reilly; Bill Carroll, Millknock; John Murphy, Broadway, brother of the famous Munn and Bertie, father of teacher Ita Cullen, Ballycogley; Jim Doyle, The Chour; Peter Marley, Kisha; Nick Doyle,. The Chour; Peter Carroll, Butlerstown; Paddy Redmond, Hilltown, Tacumshane, the last survivor, former President of the Wexfordmen's Association in New York and a familiar, active figure, in south Wexford; Jack Ellard, Carne; Bill Carthy of Airdownes, and John Waters of Ballymitty.

Four members of Cumann na mBan at an IRA training camp at Ballytrent during the Truce of 1922. Only the two ladies at the back can be identified. Left, Eileen Cotter and beside her Dorothy Dillon of Harpoonstown, Bridgetown, who later was a Gaelic League Irish teacher and national school teacher. She married Laurence Roche of Scar, Duncormick, himself a leading Sinn Fein activist at the time. *(Richard Roche Collection)*

BALLYTRENT
TRAINING CAMP

Showing a rifle, side-arm and ammunition bandolier is a member of Cumann na mBan at Ballytrent IRA camp during the Truce. She is wearing one of the newly issued provisional government army soft caps. Most of these girls took the anti-treaty side in the Civil War 1922-23. The uniforms were only used subsequently by the Free State soldiers.
(Richard Roche Collection)

Eileen Cotter of Cumann na mBan in newly issued uniform and rifle at Ballytrent training camp during the truce. *(Richard Roche Collection)*

A member of Cumann na mBan undergoing arms training near Ryans of Ballytrent House. Ballytrent itself with its massive early rath or earth works has been connected with torrents of political manoeuvre from earliest times to the 1798 rising and subsequently with the political Redmond family, the Talbots and Augustus Welby Pugin in residence. The Ballytrent Truce period photos suggest that arms bearing women might very likely be needed.
(Courtesy of Dillon family, Harpoonstown).

Cumann na mBan member Eileen Cotter (left) and another at the Ballytrent IRA camp.
(Richard Roche Collection)

Another huge advertisement proclaimed:

Michael Collins during his visit to Wexford as Minister for Finance. He was invited to pose with the sturdy Pierce bicycle, as every visitor of massive promotional importance was asked to do. Following his killing at Beal na mBlath the photo was never used again and lay for many years in Pierce's boardroom drawer. It resurfaced in 1967.

MICHAEL COLLINS IN WEXFORD

It was the ninth of April, 1922, about ten weeks before the outbreak of civil war. Wexford papers of that time provided evidence of the atmosphere. The confusion, idealism. heart searching and bitterness groaned from every page.

From The People Newspapers April 7th. A large clearly written warning:

Mick Collins, with the fateful signing and years of war behind him, arrived in Wexford on Saturday, April 8th, 1922. He stayed in the Talbot Hotel and on the following morning visited the huge centre of the Irish Agricultural Machinery Industry at Pierces in which, as the new Minister of Finance, he had a vital interest. At the time Pierces also manufactured bedsteads, threshing machines and a huge range of bicycles. A Pierce bike was presented to the Big Fellow by Philip Pierce.

The Sunday of April 9th was a violent one. It lashed rain all day with claps of thunder rolling. The section of the army opposed to the Treaty determined to turn the event into a fiasco.

The special train left Dublin with a thousand on board. At Woodenbridge, the railway line was completely torn up. All passengers disembarked and railway workers were assembled to get the train under way. "Armed men" immediately grabbed their tools and flung them into the river. The train eventually got under way but at Enniscorthy the driver was taken away by the "Armed Men". A protesting passenger was made to apologise to the "Armed Men" on his knees, in the rain and with revolvers pointing at him.

Trains disrupted

The Waterford line on the other side of Wexford was also in trouble. Both the Cork-Rosslare Express and the Waterford Pro-Treaty Special were thrown into the chaos that was Wexford that Sunday. Again the railway was repaired but it was found that the telegraph wires had been cut and the train retraced to New Ross, whereupon with firm speed the driver and fireman were arrested by the "Armed Men" and "taken outside the town". They were returned after a few hours and the train made back to Waterford. Rails were removed on every conceivable rail approach to Wexford. At Ross 70 people had their ticket money refunded.

The situation was the same on the New Ross-Wexford Road where trees were felled by the score. Captain P. J. Mackey and other men of the local company cleaned away every one of them and afterwards issued this statement to the press: "The blocking of roads, holding up of trains and the commandeering of Mr. Taylor the vet's car were all unofficial deeds and I strongly disapprove of such methods. I believe in freedom of speech for all sides. No member of the New Ross Company had anything to do with it. In my opinion such methods are calculated to advance the treaty and be no good to the republican cause".

Of the Specials only the Gorey one arrived in time for the meeting. The Dublin train with exasperated passengers arrived two hours after the meeting and five hours after the scheduled time.

An immense throng filled St. Peter's Square and the Redmondstown Band played national airs. On the platform with Michael Collins stood the chairman, Mr. J. J. Stafford, Ald. Dick Corish, M.C.C., J. J. O'Byrne, M.C.C., E. P. Foley, Michael Doyle, M.C.C., Thomas McCarthy, U.D.C., Enniscorthy; William Doyle, Andrew Doyle, L. Cummins, T.C.; Thos Hayes, T.C.; Pat Morris, P.L.G.; James F. McCarthy, P. J. Gregory, S. A. O'Leary, M. O'Connor, Philip Pierce, D. Sears, T. O'Dunbar, M. Hassett and two ladies, Misses Kathleen Browne and M. Furlong, all of whom were prominent in the national, political and business life of the county.

Passionate oratory

Mick Collins, with his burning personality and passionate oratory, was the centre of attraction and the terrible struggle was demonstrated in his word, his face and frame, his gestures.

"Freedom is not a question of a form of Government. Ireland suffered the greatest oppression of all under the Republic of Cromwell. In the free exercise of these sovereign rights without interference it is not the treaty that matters. It is not a document solution that matters. It is the departure of British troops that matters. It is this departure that makes us free from their interference, this departure is the one indispensable factor in our freedom. No good can come of a division among ourselves, from civil war, from mutiny, from indiscipline in the Army, from using part of the Army as a political machine. There is no reason why these things should be. Can we not cease to look for the mean motive in every word uttered by each of us and look instead for the generous one. Can we not agree to disagree where we disagree, to unite for objects common to us all? Let us be patriots before we are partisans. For if this fight must be resumed the whole world will look on".

Collins attended the 11 o'clock Sunday Mass in the Franciscan Church, accompanied by Mr. James J. Stafford, Alderman Richard Corish, T.D. (Mayor) and Mr. S. A. O'Leary. He was subsequently received at the convent by the Guardian, Fr. Peter, OFM. He also visited Mrs. Furlong whose son had been killed in the War of Independence.

Collins was followed by Alderman Dick Corish, Mayor of Wexford, a great conductor of the masses, another great orator: "We have heard a lot about a republic". Voice: "You'll hear more about it." "I hope I will but there is a lot more talking about it today that weren't talking about it twelve months ago." Voice: "Where were you in 1916." "I was in jail in 1916." (cheers).

And so on and on in the drenching rain with no one leaving for shelter and the saturated Michael Collins examining the faces. Then it was over and the sodden crowd dispersed. It was the last time Michael Collins was in Wexford. In four months his corpse became one of the most bitterly regretted sacrifices in Cogadh na gCaraid–the War of the Friends. In 1922 on July 7, the first Wexford casualty of the Civil War died from a shotgun blast in Monck Street.

Enniscorthy Flying Column, Carnew 1922, a photograph taken after the Truce declaration and before the Civil War. Some of the Volunteers have been issued with new army uniforms.

COLLINS MEETS LEADING CITIZENS

Michael Collins met business and political leaders on April 9, 1922. He was Minister for Finance. The farm machinery industry in Wexford was vital to the Co. Wexford and Irish economy so he visited the centres of manufacturing. A group photograph was taken outside Pierces offices where Michael Collins was formally photographed, almost certainly by Charles Vize, with the political, commercial and trade union interests involved.

In front: Dr. William P. Hearne, LI.D; Managing Director Wexford Engineering Co., Ltd. (Star IronWorks); Alderman Richard Corish, Mayor of Wexford; Philip Pierce, Managing Director, Philip Pierce and Co. Ltd.; Michael Collins, Minister for Finance, William Doyle and his brother Andrew Doyle, owner directors of Doyle's Selskar Ironworks; unidentified.

Middle row: Thomas Hayes, Wexford Corporation, Lawrence Cummins, Wexford Corporation; unidentified, unidentified, Joseph Mulally (former famed All-Ireland football championship goal-keeper), a painter by profession.

Back row: unidentified, Thomas Barnes, Wexford Engineering Ltd., posssibly James J. Stafford, Cromwellsfort, probably T. W. Salmon, Manager, Pierces; unidentified, unidentified.

Before lunching in the Talbot Hotel, Collins was presented with a beautiful set of Irish-made pipes. He was a pipe connoisseur and handed the case of pipes to one of his bodyguards saying, "I don't want anyone to whip these on me". The late Mrs Bevin (Bev) Leahy (nee Morrissey), St. Ibar's Villas, granddaughter of Bessie Doyle, was the young girl chosen to make the presentation to Collins. She was accompanied by the Misses Kathleen Browne, Mary Furlong, Maeve Gregory and Mrs Matt O'Connor, all members of Cumann na Saoirse.

Photo taken outside Pierce's foundry office.

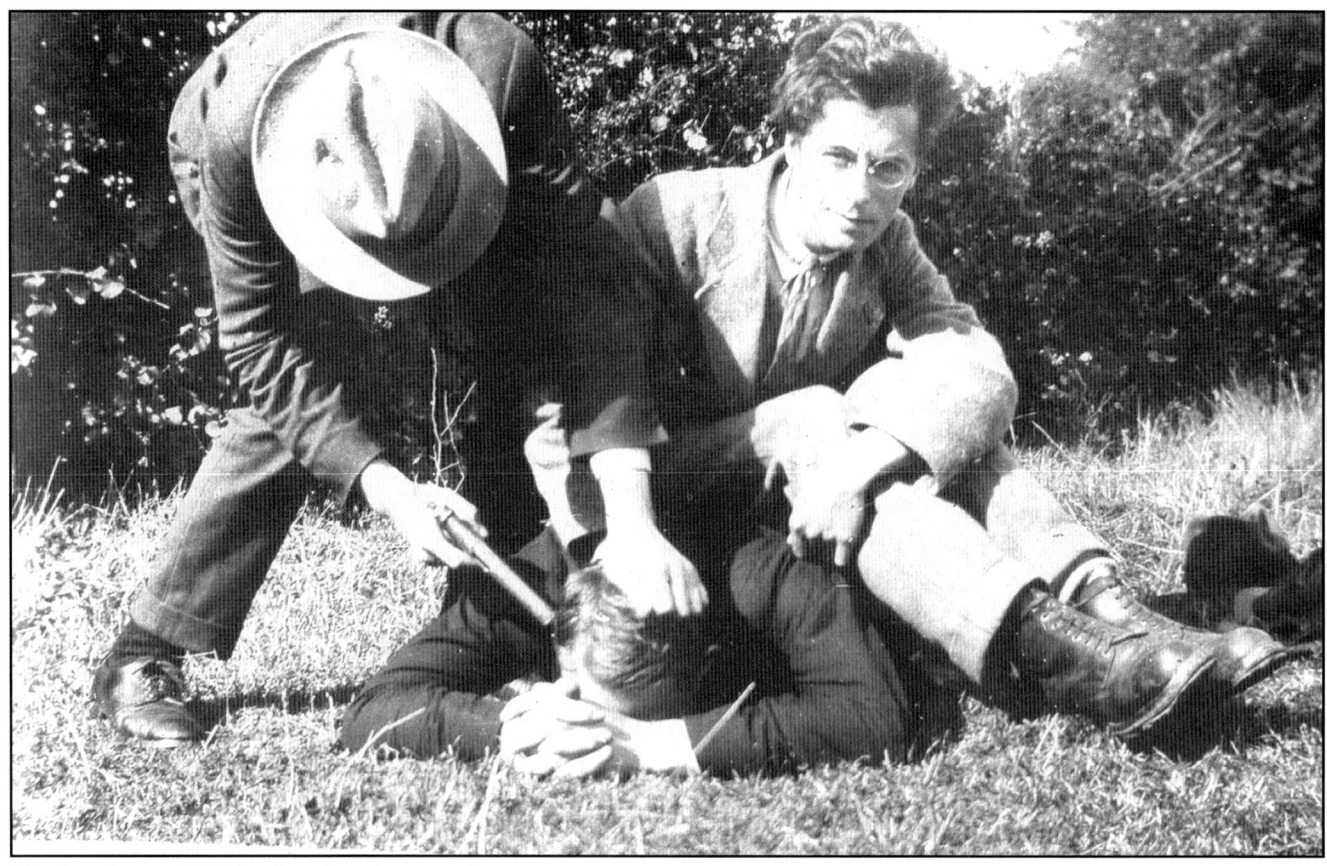

"Acting the goat". This alarming photograph
of IRA fighters play-acting during the Truce
was certainly taken, posed, in Duncannon.
(Sinnott Collection)

REST AND PLAY AT
DUNCANNON

More posed Truce period
clowning. This time it is "Pax"
Sinnott with the revolver.

(Sinnott Collection)

"Pax" Sinnott, at left, with two I.R.A. field
soldiers at Duncannon's quayside during the
Truce 1921. *(Sinnott Collection)*

"Pax" Sinnott, at left, with two volunteers and a
revolver. It is probable that the photos were snapped by
"Pax" Sinnott's later wife, Máirín Heery in
Duncannon.

(Sinnott Collection)

Kathleen Browne of Rathronan Castle, writer, historian, Irish Irelander, former prisoner in Kilmainham Jail, found time to enjoy her favourite sport, riding side saddle with the Killinick Harriers. *(Photo courtesy Bernard Browne)*

Relaxed, posed and defiant. A dressed unit with tricolour and bayonet. This photo from the Shane Sinnott collection has no details attached.

The Irish Republican Army soldiers in their first general issue uniforms. The photo was taken in Kilkenny. The soldiers are from C. Company, South Wexford Brigade. First: kneeling at left, is Nick Roche who many will remember as the long term caretaker of Wexford G.A.A. Park in Clonard. At extreme right, same row, Tom Duffin, Wexford. We cannot be certain of the other names. The lack of formality shows that it was taken well before the Civil War outbreak, while the reclining officer seem to indicate that they are waiting for the official photo to be posed.

(Photo courtesy Elsie Dempsey, nee Roche).

Anti-Treaty meeting in Duncannon, 1922.
(Sinnott Collection)

Officers and men of the Royal Irish Constabulary photographed by Charles E. Vize in their George Street Barracks, Wexford, now Pembroke House. This group photo was taken before their disbandment in 1922.

Mary McSwiney, sister of Terence McSwiney, Lord Mayor of Cork who died on hunger strike, addresses an anti-Treaty rally at the Tholsel in New Ross.

Crowd scene at the anti-Treaty rally addressed by Mary McSwiney in New Ross. *(Photos courtesy Paddy Berry)*

The newly uniformed Irish Republican Army soldiers, probably locals, make their first appearance in Clonegal, summer 1922.

The photograph from the Senator Kathleen Browne collection shows newly uniformed IRA veterans before the outbreak of the Civil War. The difference between the faces here and the faces of young recruits into the Free State army is striking, particularly the comparatively elderly soldier with his cap on his knees, seated first from the right. The presence of the contented dog indicates that it's the Browne pet but it is most likely that the soldiers were local. If the situation had not been tragic the address of an officer in Wexford Barracks square would be amusing. All units of the IRA in the field or resting were called on parade. They were clad in the newly issued green uniforms. The officer addressed them abruptly: "Those of you who want to remain in the army stand at ease. Those of you for the heather hills of Ireland fall out."

Take-over. Immediately the orders to the British Army to evacuate came into effect, I.R.A. soldiers were promptly switched to security duties. Our photograph shows Daniel Jevens on guard at the entrance to Dublin's City Hall. The banner at the back declares change, "Eire's First Guard," with a diagram of the G.P.O. upon it. Daniel Jevens was one of Michael Collins' special forces. He was transferred to the Active Service Unit which dealt with British Intelligence agents when the War of Independence intensified. They were given the nom-de-guerre, "The Twelve Apostles". He was wounded in action. On 3 March 1922, he was attached to A Company, Beggars Bush Barracks, Dublin. He was father of Captain Daniel Jevens, Irish Army, Dolcordon, Coolcotts (formerly Jevens, Jewellers, 84 South Main St, Wexford and F.C.A. Wexford Barracks.)
(Photo from Capt. Daniel Jevens)

Two Wexford veterans in Ireland's new army before the Civil War outbreak. They have freshly issued uniforms, rifles, greatcoats, leggings, ammunition belts and soft caps.

A group of Free State officers in County Wexford before Civil War hostilities opened. The civilian is probably a fellow officer out of uniform. As IRA soldiers in the field arrived to barracks evacuated by the British Army they were asked on parade if they would serve in the Free State Army. No pressure was exerted to remain. All the men were at liberty to choose sides.

Two proud I.R.A. soldiers in their newly issued National Army uniforms, 1922. They later took the anti-treaty side in the Civil War and had to discard the uniforms rapidly, a common occcurence when hostilities opened and opposing sides were taken in June 1922. Seated on left: Patrick Kennedy, Shielbaggan, who later worked the family farm until his death. Standing: Willie Anglim, Saltmills, who later took up residence in Wexford, where he married. He worked for the firm of Traynors, with whom, for many years, he was a lorry driver. He died about 1980.

(With thanks to Patricia Silkstone, editor On the Hook, Poulfur 1995)

Wexford District Council, taken probably by Charles Vize, before December 6th, 1921. The date is important. It was during the period of the Truce. Civil War broke out the following year. Standing, left to right: Mr. Codd, Ballymore; James Ennis, Ford of Lyng; Tom Cousins, Rathaspeck, our donor's father. Tom Cousins in addition to being a public body political activist, was also an officer in the South Wexford Brigade of the IRA throughout the War of Independence. Dick Dillon of The Moor, Mulrankin; unidentified, M. M. Roche, Kilmore; unidentified. Seated with either a plate blemish or cigarette is another we cannot identify. Next, Larry Mahon, Carne; Chris Culleton, Ringaheen, chairman, sire of all the Culletons including our adviser Joe, and Heritage Park , Dr. Ned. The orator, Willie Boggan of Whiterock, is next, and in our opinion the low sized figure at the end is Nicholas Greene of Wexford town. In front Willie Doyle of Bridgetown but we cannot identify the substantial figure alongside him.

England supporters at Dublin's North Wall as the British Army evacuates in 1922 to musical accompaniment at the rear.
(Shane Sinnott Collection)

A group mostly of younger recruits to the newly formed Free State Army. The photo is from the Kathleen Browne Collection so we must assume that it is the lady herself, an indefatigable and life-long Irish-Irelander, giving the lesson. She was already a much published historian.

The Civil War, the "liberation of Ireland", the pro-Treaty and anti-Treaty General Election campaigns were covered with special interest in defeated Germany. This striking photo of General Richard Mulcahy addressing a pro-Treaty rally made the front cover of the Munich Illustrated Press.
(Mulcahy Collection)

1901. This photograph of seemingly modest claim to fame carries nevertheless a significant flavour. The photograph was taken by Charles Vize before his later prominence as a professional photographer. He has, however, posed his subjects carefully. The photograph was taken in Oylegate at the fresh-air presentation of medals to the Kruger G.A.A. club committee members. Kruger was the President of the Boer Republic of South Africa during the Boer War at the turn of the century. Reflecting on the Fenian submission that England's difficulty was Ireland's opportunity the club called itself after England's enemy. The Boer resistance to Britain's Imperial Army roused sympathy all over the world. Yet another G.A.A. club, Campile, named their team as the "Free Staters" after one of the Boer republics, the Orange Free State. It was to have a different interpretation later in 1922-23. *(Bernard Browne Collection)*

SPORT

Despite the terrible violence which claimed the decade, Co. Wexford created an unsurpassed record in sport. In 1910 the first senior All-Ireland hurling trophy was won. From 1913 to 1918 Wexford's senior footballers won six Leinster titles in a row. They contested seven All-Ireland football finals, one of which was drawn, and they won four consecutive All-Ireland senior football championships. In 1918 the county achieved the remarkable accolade of playing in both All-Ireland finals, football and hurling. The hurlers were smitten by the prevailing flu and lost heavily to Limerick. The football record has never been surpassed.

The horse industry and 'sport of kings' made progress. There was an insatiable demand by the British army for cavalry horses throughout the war. They were bought by agents and collected on the South Sloblands among other centres. There their mouths were examined by army veterinaries before being declared suitable. Unscrupulous horse dealers could not resist the temptation to "rejuvenate" horses mouths by extracting teeth, well before inspection by the British Army agents. It must be recorded, however, that while all sports thrived, sport also separated people on class, ethnic, social and religious lines, a situation which is not noticeable to the same extent at all in the present century.

The only surviving photo of the Gorey Wolfe Tones hurling team, champions of Co. Wexford 1907. Defiant looking men, even their title had defiance for the national upsurges were still a decade away. The photo was taken in the Fidlers Field, Clonattin, Gorey, and the identifiable spectators crowding around the team have been identified by Michael Fitzpatrick as Tom Donohoe. Mr. Keegan, Tom Murphy, Michael Doyle and Tom Redmond. The team itself is as follows,starting with the first of the seventeen men in the front row, from the left: Martin Murphy, Edward Doyle, T. Byrne, Michael Murphy, the proud and unrepentant gorsoon is Paddy "Bud" Redmond, alongside Jim Redmond. Middle row: T. Murphy, Seán Kirwan, P. O'Gara, H. Wall. The next player is the mystery man on the team, the "dark horse", unnamed, except that he is from the hurling nursery of Blackwater. (He resembles Seán Etchingham. Would that be possible?) Next is Michael Kinsella and T. Byrne. Back row: Moses Redmond, Michael Connors, Ned Breen, T. Byrne, and J.Finn. *(Michael Fitzpatrick Collection)*

The Oylegate Kruger's men.

(Photo by Charles Vize, Bernard Browne Collection)

John Barker of South Main Street, Wexford, merchant and travel agent, was married to Sarah White of Enniscorthy. John Barker, like his wife, was a Republican and an "Irish Irelander" He was probably a member of the oath-bound secret society, the Irish Republican Brotherhood. It was in John Barker's (now Asple's) drawing room that Seán T. O'Kelly, later President of Ireland, issued the oath to all members of the recruited IRB in Wexford.

John Barker was one of the dynamic figures in the G.A.A. administration of the 1913 to 1918 Co. Wexford senior football, record-breaking, four-in-a-row team. That was not all. He was one of the giant and most successful oarsmen in Ireland, a man indispensable to the Wexford Boat Club crews. And John Barker loved the sport.

However, in Nationalist eyes, whether Redmondite or Sinn Féin, the Wexford Harbour Boat Club was regarded as a nest of active anti-nationalists, or if you prefer, Unionists. John Barker was "on the spot" although he often laughed heartily about it. Several of his antagonists wanted to expel him from the G.A.A. unless he severed his connection with the boat club. He argued his point so well that the matter was "shelved". Our photo under the newspaper heading "The Winning Crew" shows, seated from left, John Barker and Patrick G. O'Connor who was an eminent citizen and builder. Standing, J. Huggard, solr., Lower Rowe Street (cox), George Ashmore, and Michael Kavanagh. Michael Kavanagh, was the father of Michael Kavanagh former garden and light machinery business director in The Bull Ring and John Street, Wexford.

The newspaper report states glowingly, "We have pleasure in presenting our readers with a picture of the Wexford Harbour Boat Club Four who are rowing so splendidly and successfully this year and who have been the first in a long time to bring back an aquatic victory to Wexford. Their cups include two won this season, the Liffey Cup won at the Metropolitan Regatta and the Pierce Cup regained by them in home waters last week." The photograph was taken by Charles Vize, cira 1916. Four of the Wexford Harbour Boat Club's Junior Four were almost unbeaten nationally in 1913-14. Four of their most accomplished rowers joined the British Army at the outbreak of war in 1914. They were all awarded officer commissions. Tim Keating and Willie O'Keefe were killed in action in France. Addison Hadden was captured by the Germans and Alphonsus Crean died shortly after the war.

The Wexford Hounds at Bricketstown House, 1909. The hunt was established by Col. Piggott, Slevoy Castle, about the beginning of the 19th century. He was master until 1848. In 1840 Capt. James Harvey, Park House, kept a pack of fox-hounds and hunted some of the county with Col. Piggott. *(Taghmon Historical Society Collection)*

The St. John's Volunteers, 1909 junior county champions. Back row left to right: Pat Rice, Michael O'Neill, Tom Boyle, Jack Murphy, Richard Brien, Mike Flusk, Stephen Murphy, Jack O'Brien, Joe Wadding, Ed O'Leary, Larry Doyle. Front row: Johnny Howlin, Mick Cogley, Pat Carroll, Tom McGrath, Rev. T. Moran, C.C., Dan Morris, Jem Whelan, Barney Roice, Owen Kehoe. Seated: Jem Driscoll, James Tyghe, Richard Hanton and James Goodison. The interesting aspect of this photo is the Vols chaplain, Fr. Moran. He was Mulgannon born, the place of the Vols club enemies, the Mulgannon Harriers. *(Courtesy Liam Lahiff)*

The 1911 Wexford District senior football final, between the Volunteers and Sarsfields played at Wexford Park. The Volunteers are wearing a new set of jerseys of Green and White in vertical stripes. In the early years the club colours were red. *(Courtesy Liam Lahiff)*

1910: New Ross Boat Club enjoyed considerable success in a remarkable decade for sport. The photograph of their Junior Eight, winners of the Harbour Commissioners Challenge Cup, Waterford and the Cooke Challenge Cup, Wexford, include the man who dominated several team sports throughout the decade and played a major role in the struggle for independence and Civil War, better known as Seán O' Kennedy. He is formally listed here as T. J. O'Kennedy. The crew are J. Crean, T. Doran, P. Hagan, J. Doyle, T. J. O'Kennedy, J. Kehoe, M. Sheehan (cox), P. Deegan (stk), P. O'Hanlon.
(Photo courtesy of New Ross Harbour Boat Club)

Another trophy for New Ross Harbour Boat Club's Eight. Seán O'Kennedy is third from left standing. *(Courtesy of New Ross Harbour Boat Club)*

Opening of Clonattin Golf Club Gorey, Circa 1916. Front row, left to right (seated): Mrs. Harvey, Duffcarrig; Mrs. Donovan, Ballymore; Miss Nora Malone, Mrs. Jackson, Bank of Ireland; Mrs. Col. Quinn, Borleigh, who presented the men's trophy; Mrs. Cantillon, National Bank; Col. W. Quinn, Borleigh; Peter Redmond (nephew of Miss Annie Redmond's), now Mace Supermarket, with cup; Mrs. Morris, Bank of Ireland; Miss Brickerton, Mrs. Thos. Doyle, Miss Kinsella, later Mrs. Mernagh. Second row : Miss Babs Hickey – aunt of Mrs. Mernagh; Danny Mullen; Miss Donovan, Ballymore; Doris Nolan, niece of Dr. Nolan, Gorey; Vincent Dwyer, Bank of Ireland; Miss Colter, C.O.I. teacher; Wm. Hargrove, Mrs. Mullins, Josie Doyle, Empire Hotel; Mrs. O'Carroll, Chemists; Lena Hargrove, Miss O'Brien, visitor from Edenderry; D.J. Bolger, Millmount; Mr. Jackson, Bank of Ireland; Mr. Williamson, Bank of Ireland. Back row: Dr. Dwyer, Bridie Doyle, 80 Main St.; Nancy Byrne, Ballycale; Mr. Morris, Aidan Mernagh, Peter Redmond (won men's trophy), Miss Cantillon won ladies trophy. *(Michael Fitzpatrick Collection)*

The handclasp of legends. "Tearin' Tom" Doyle of Ballyhogue, the Wexford captain, shakes hands with the famous Kerry captain, Dick Fitzgerald of Killarney, before the throw-in for the 1913 All-Ireland Senior Football Final between Wexford and Kerry at Jones Road (Croke Park).

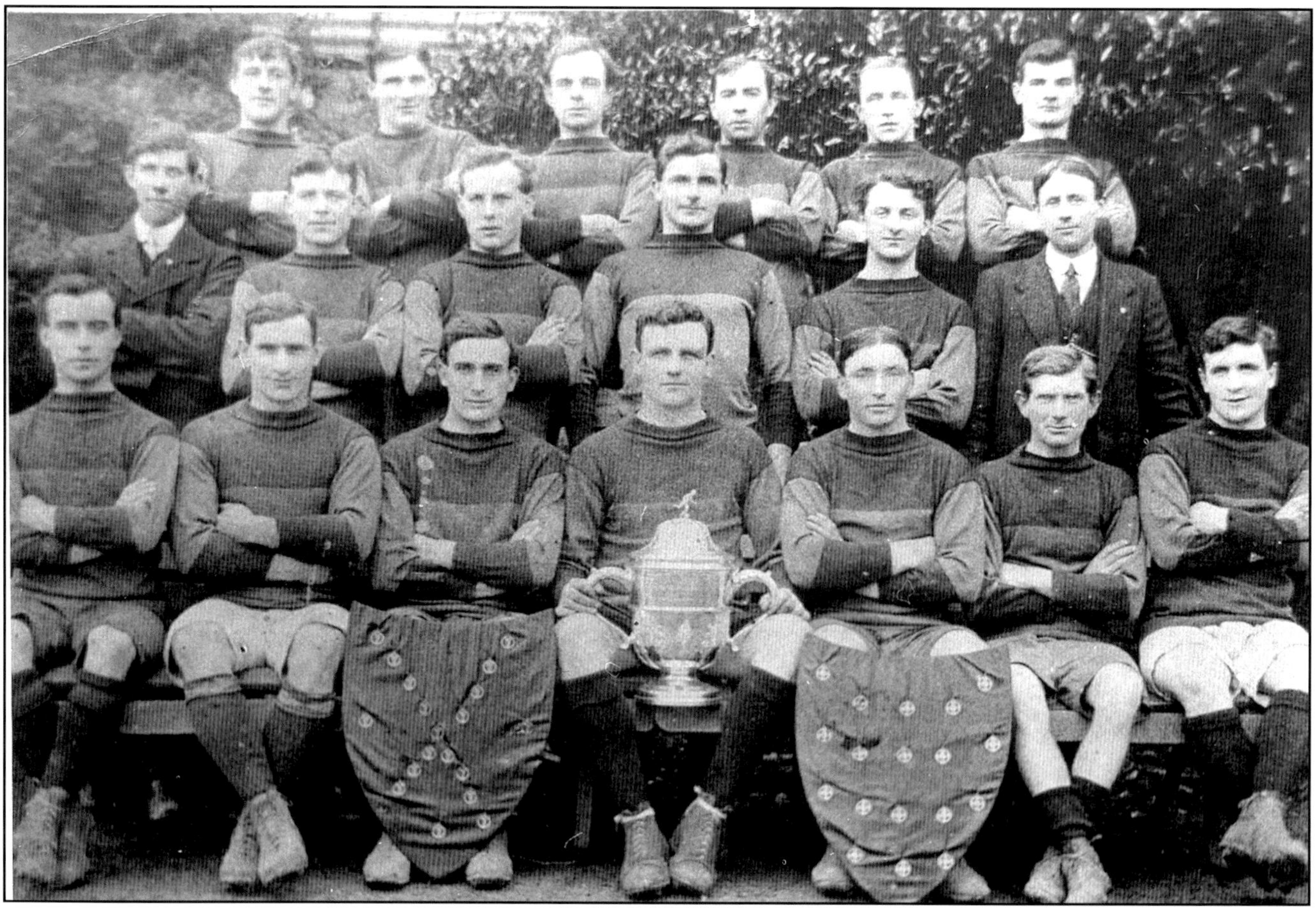

Wexford All-Ireland senior football champions, 1918. A special photograph taken after Wexford's four-in-a-row was completed. Back row (l-r): John Wall (Bunclody), Frank Furlong (Wexford), Rich Reynolds (Wexford), Tom Mernagh (New Ross), Val Connolly (Enniscorthy), Jack Crowley (Wexford). Middle: Denis Asple, selector (Ballyhogue), Tom Doyle (Ballyhogue), Martin Howlett (Compile), Father E. Wheeler (Wexford), P.J. Mackey (New Ross), P.D. Breen, selector (Castlebridge). Front: Tom Murphy (Enniscorthy), T. McGrath (Wexford), Jim Byrne (Wexford), captain 1918; Seán O'Kennedy (New Ross), captain 1915, '16 and '17; Aidan Doyle (New Ross), B. Roice (Wexford), Gus O'Kennedy (New Ross), Ned Black (Enniscorthy).

James Davis of Walshestown, Master of the Killinick Harriers, with pack and farmer huntsmen. At left James Codd, Moorfield, who was so enthusiastic that he followed the hunt on a bicycle, and John Rossiter of Brookfield with his favourite grey.

(Photo Nicholas Kelly)

Although dealt with in previous volumes it would be unacceptable to omit the successes which had the county's population thrilled from end to end of the decade. One participant informed this writer that until 1917 huge crowds met the hurlers and footballers at the railway stations after every triumph. So frequent was annual All-Ireland victory however, by 1917 and 1918 the welcoming crowds had dwindled. The hurlers, stricken by the influenza outbreak, were however heavily beaten by Limerick. Our photo of the 1918 hurling team (showing some damage) was taken by Cashmans of Dublin before the Leinster Senior Hurling final when Wexford beat Dublin's "League of Nations" selection by 2 - 3 to 1 - 2. Standing: P. D. Breen (County President G.A.A.); M. Stafford, Jim Fogarty, Dick Walshe, Sean Kennedy (mentor) Michael O'Leary, Paddy Lambert, P. McCullough (County Secretary). Seated: J. Fortune, Dave Kavanagh, Paddy Roche, J. O'Leary, Michael Cummins (captain), J. Sinnott, Mick Neville, and M. Murphy. In front: P. Fagan, T. Murphy, R. Lambert and J. Devereux. Robert Lambert later became one of the most active IRA flying column commanders. He played at full forward in the 1918 All-Ireland hurling final against Limerick. *(Photo, Liam Griffin Collection)*

Seated on the Croke Park sideline in jovial mood were Arthur Griffith, founder of Sinn Féin, Eamon de Valera, Laurence O'Neill, Lord Mayor of Dublin, and Michael Collins. The referee was Harry Boland (below right). *(Shane Sinnott Collection)*

On Sunday, 6 April, 1919, All-Ireland champions Wexford played Tipperary at Croke Park in a repeat of the 1918 All-Ireland football final. The proceeds were in aid of dependants of those detained in British prisons. The ball was thrown in by Eamon de Valera, President of Sinn Féin. Tipperary had been the shock team of 1918. They had overwhelmed mighty Kerry in the Munster championships and beaten Mayo in the All-Ireland semi-final. Rich Reynolds, the star Wexford forward, recalled that the Croke Park crowd were so in favour of underdog Tipp that they booed the Wexford team on All-Ireland day. Wexford won their fourth title in a row. In that tense time when the so called "foreign games" were regarded as garrison games, the ban against "foreign" game players became a matter of strict Sinn Fein security. Dr. Toddy Pierce of Wexford, a brilliant sportsman in several sports including rowing, rugby and Gaelic football, played for Wexford in 1918 as "Pierce Todd." He also won an All-Ireland medal with Dublin.

St. Anne's hurling team. Winners 1924-25 Co. Wexford Senior Hurling League (medals and cup). Back row: Thomas Kelly, James Dillon, Nicholas Parle, Walter Doyle, John Walsh, Nicholas Furlong, Patrick O'Keeffe, William Doyle.

Middle row: Francis Murphy, James O'Keeffe, James Byrne, Gregory Devereux, Thomas O'Keeffe, John Doyle, Michael Cullen.

Front row: Aidan Murphy, James Murphy, Partrick Doyle, Francis Cullen. Inset: Richard Cleary. Photo Charles Vize.

This typically clear Vize photograph had political as well as sporting significance. The enemies of the Civil War started meeting on the playing fields. Several members of the St. Anne' team had taken part in the War of Independence and then the Civil War, mostly on the Republican side, James Dillon, Walter Doyle, Patrick O'Keeffe, William Doyle, Thomas O'Keeffe, Patrick Doyle. The referee for the final William Doyle, Thomas O'Keeffe, Patrick Doyle. The referee for the final was the greatest Wexford sporting legend, War of Independence veteran and prominent Free State army combattant, Seán O'Kennedy of New Ross.

(Séamus O'Keeffe Collection)

St. Anne's hurling team, 1924

Referee Seán O'Kennedy

VISIT OF THE PRINCE ROYAL OF SAUDI ARABIA

This historic photograph was taken on 9 November 1919 on the occasion of the visit of the young Crown Prince of Saudi Arabia, Faisal Ibn Saud, with his retinue. He was a guest of M. J. O'Connor, solicitor and with him spent a shooting holiday on the famous Slob wild-life grounds. The photograph was taken at Michael O'Connor's shooting lodge at North Slob, Wexford.

Standing, left to right, are H. St. John Philby of the British Colonial Office; a cousin of the prince royal, Prince Abadulla of Qusaib; Michael J. O'Connor is seated in centre; Mrs. O'Connor is seated in front with two of the four permanently armed bodyguards. Two ladies behind, on either side of the Prince Royal Ibn Saud, are Miss Joan O'Connor and Mrs. Catherine O'Connor. St. John Philby was Britain's greatest expert on Arab and middle-eastern affairs. He was much decorated and had a thorough command of Arab languages and history. Unfortunately, he has become better known to this generation as father of the comprehensive Soviet spy master and "traitor", Kim Philby.

(F. M. O'Connor Collection)

Kim Philby

The O'Connor ladies with the young Crown Prince of Arabia.
(F. M. O'Connor Collection).

This grouping shows the youth and size of the ill-fated Faisal Ibn Saud at the time of his holiday in Wexford. There was justification for his long remembered bodyguards. King Faisal Ibn Saud's life was ended by assassins bullets on March 25, 1975.
(F. M. O'Connor Collection)

Tobacco plantation at Mount St. Benedict, Gorey

DOM SWEETMAN OF MOUNT ST. BENEDICT, GOREY

GOD'S ACRE

When the Benedictine, Dom John Francis Sweetman died in 1953 he was an established controversial figure. Born near Clohamon in 1872, Sweetman was educated at Downside Abbey, Bath, where he joined the Benedictine Order. While studying for the priesthood in Rome he displayed an independence of mind which later in life was to lead him to trouble. At the start of the Boer War Fr. Sweetman joined the British Army as chaplain. In South Africa he crossed the lines on many occasions to learn about the growing of tobacco. When he returned he promoted its cultivation in the interest of a self sufficient Ireland and a sturdy farm based industry.

The first school he opened was near Enniscorthy, but soon after he founded Mount St. Benedict. The Mount was bought with money lent to Downside by a cousin of Fr. Sweetman's. John Sweetman of Drumboragh gave the sum of £5,000 to buy the estate. This John Sweetman was one of the founder members of Sinn Féin.

For a time the Mount did flourish as a public school. John Dillon (leader of the Irish Parliamentary Party) sent four of his five sons, including James, to be educated there. Also there as students were The O'Rahilly, Nobel Peace Prize winner Seán McBride, Fintan O'Connor, solicitor, the Wexford Sweetmans of course, and the author Dr. James Deeney, late of Rathdowney, Rosslare, with many other noted

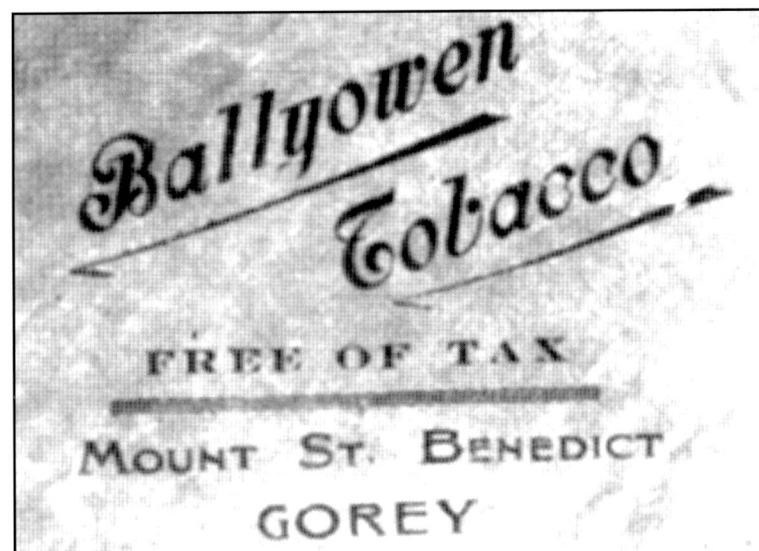

contributors to Irish life.

The tobacco was a bitter-smelling item and even worse to smoke, but at that time people were not so fussy about their brand and acquired tastes for things more bitter than Fr. Sweetman's tobacco. When the Government heard of this new venture they sent down Tax Commissioners to collect a half≤penny for every pound's worth (sterling) sold. Fr. Sweetman, being the stubborn man he was, refused to hear of such an idea. The tobacco was drawn from the surrounding sheds and burned in front of the house.

The passing years and political climate changed Fr. Sweetman's attitudes towards Britain and by 1916 he was supporting the Anti-Conscription campaign. In 1917 he defiantly attended the huge funeral tribute to the Irish Volunteer leader, Thomas Ashe, hunger striker, who died during force feeding.

With rebel attitudes and revolutionary ideas pressure closed around him. In 1919 the bishop of Ferns, Dr. Codd, asked the Abbot of Downside to close the school. The Abbot refused and the bishop appealed to Rome. The dispute that followed was long. In 1923 Rome rejected Dr. Codd's appeal to close the school but ordered a new superior to be placed in charge. Fr.

A label from the tobacco carton

Thomas Ashe, lying in state, 1917.

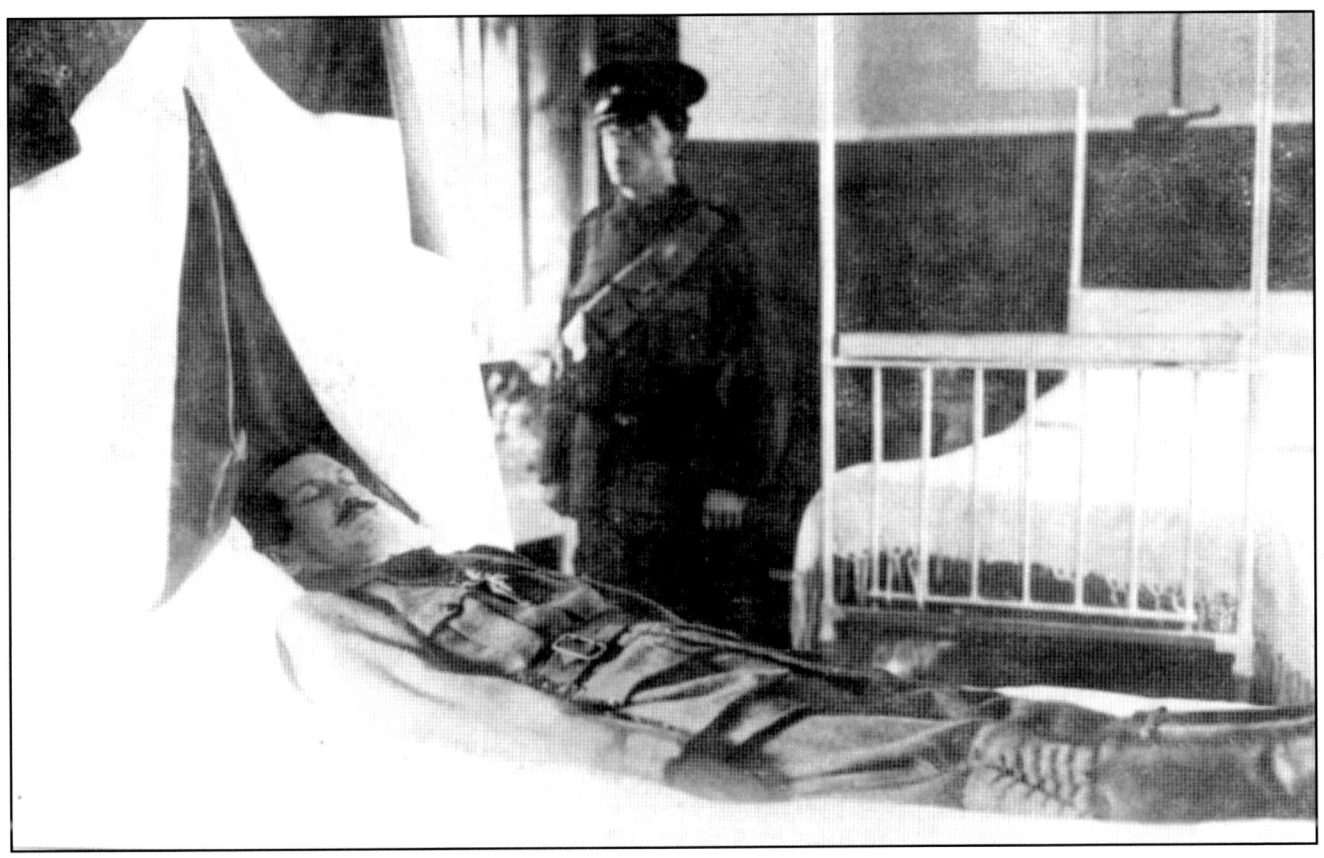

Dom Sweetman and staff members at Mount St. Benedict, Hollyfort, Gorey: Misses Brennan, Levingstone, Devitt, Mrs Ryan and Miss Kehoe
(Michael Fitzpatrick Collection)

Dom Sweetman of Mount St. Benedict

Sweetman, gave in because of his love for the place. He retired to work in Liverpool. When word got to him of a plan that the Abbot of Downside had to sell it, he returned to Ireland in defiance of the Abbot to defend his own creation.

Trouble heaped on trouble. He was summoned to Rome, accused of harbouring IRA soldiers during the civil war. He was also accused of sanctioning their recruitment in the Mount. He claimed if anything such had happened he knew nothing about it. When he arrived home in Gorey he was greeted by hundreds of cheering followers who placed him in a coach and drew the whole four miles distance to the Mount. Long before he died, Fr. Sweetman formed his own burial committee in order to ensure his remains would be buried in the grave of his choice on the Mount land. The burial committee included, Malachy Sweetman, Paddy Redmond, the late William "Bill" Brennan who excavated and covered more graves than any other man in the Parish of Craanford, and other local men, who were faithful supporters of Fr. Sweetman.

On the day following Fr. Sweetman's death, an order came from Downside to have the priest's remains flown to England for burial in the Abbey Cemetery at Downside. That sparked off some heated controversy, but in the end the committee, backed by the local people won the day and the remains of the beloved Headmaster, drawn by farm horse-cart, were buried in the grave he had marked, in a lonely little "spinney" in one of the Mount fields, known as the "The Fourteen Acres."

1953: Wishes honoured. Dom Sweetman's remains are taken by the farm horse and cart to his winter place of rest in Mount St. Benedict's land. The wellington boots on the horse leader are eloquent of the conditions. The chief family mourner is Roger Sweetman of Ballycourcy. Behind him in impeccable formal dress is the President of Ireland, Seán T. O'Ceallaigh, his aid-de-camp and a concourse of his loyal friends and neighbours.

The Very Rev. Thomas Brownell Gibson, Dean of Ferns, 1908 -1926. He entered Trinity College in 1873, and during his undergraduate course he was engaged in tuition. Among his pupils were Sir Horace Plunkett and Lord Dunsany. He was ordained priest in 1877 and served as Chaplain and Head Master of Kings Hospital, Dublin, 1877-96, after which he bacame Rector of Kilbride and Ferns. He was a noted educationalist. His writings included "Jottings from a Parish Register". He died 19 January 1927 and was buried in Ferns. There is a window to his memory in Ferns Cathedral.

A RELIGIOUSLY
REBELLIOUS CHOIR

While this choir photograph has the appearance of proper tranquillity it contains startling evidence of a shift in feelings inside one year. The male voice choir of St. Peter's College Seminary had won a major prize in Feis Charman, May 1917. The 1916 Rising, the executions and he imprisonments had traumatic effect on attitudes in Nationalist Ireland of every shade. However for a seminary group to be formally photographed by the firm of Charles Vize, Wexford and Enniscorthy, in 1917, proclaiming the Irish Republic openly was audacity taken to unprecedented levels. At the back, held proudly upwards by two stalwarts, is a "home-made" banner, orange, white and green, with a shamrock imposed and the ominous

initials I.R.– Irish Republic.

Authorised or unauthorised? We will never know, but the photographic record stands. Most of the singers are from various parts of Ireland but the few Diocese of Ferns men in it were alive and famed in living memory. The men (the Roman collar indicates a deacon) at back are M. J. O'Ryan and J. McCorry holding the banner.

The third row has Murdoch Keating of Yoletown, Broadway, later C.C. Wexford and New Ross, and P.P. Craanford; P. Quilligan; P. Kiernan; Martin Kinsella, Carnew, later P.P. Kilmuckridge; M. Moore and A. Power.

Second row, Nicholas Cardiff, noted singer and cantor, violinist and Gaelic League worker. Born in Gurteenminogue, Murrintown, he served as a priest in London, Wexford, Rosslare and later as Parish Priest in Ballyoughter; M. Colgan, D. Godfrey, J. Tagney, J. Doherty, W. Geaney, M O'Kennedy, M. McHugh, P. S. Ray and P. J. McArdle.

Seated, Michael Rossiter, Brookfield, Rathaspeck who died as P.P.

Craanford; Patrick Browne of Ballywilliam, who later served Askamore, Courtnacuddy, Trinity and Barntown. Alongside him is one of the most famous of all, Edward Wheeler. A native of Killurin, after ordination he served in Cushinstown, Caim, Clongeen, Tinahely, Kilmuckridge and Bree. He was one of the greatest footballers in Ireland in the first half of the twentieth century helping Wexford to six Leinster senior titles in a row, four All-Ireland titles in a row 1915, '16, '17 and '18, a record never surpassed.

Strictly forbidden to leave or take part in sports outside the seminary, he was repeatedly "smuggled" out, sometimes disguised as a woman. He played under the assumed names of "James Furlong", "E. Phelan" and "J. Quinn". He was the best fullback in Ireland and had an uncanny understanding with the equally brilliant Wexford goalie, Tom McGrath. It is hard to credit that the seminary superiors or Bishop Browne did not know about Edward Wheeler's assisted strategies. It is easier to believe that they did, but turned a blind eye.

Next to E. Wheeler is Rev. J. D. Gerrard, conductor of the choir; P. J. Codd, choir organiser; T. O'Brien and Michael Kelly of Ballyellis – he later became Dean in St. Peter's College and Professor of Church History. His health failed and he died in the college at 42 years of age.

John Allen Fitzgerald Gregg, Church of Ireland Bishop of Ferns 1915-1920. In wartime he invited controversy by signing a nationwide protest against Ireland's partition. In 1920 he was elected Archbishop of Dublin. He was sometimes in amusing difficulty because of his uncanny resemblance to Eamon de Valera. They later became firm friends though Bishop Gregg was a firm but benign Unionist. An outstanding and famed scholar, he was appointed to the short-lived Senate envisaged by the government of Ireland Act, 1920. In 1938 he was elected Archbishop of Armagh and Church of Ireland Primate of All Ireland.

Bishop James Browne of Bigbarn, Mayglass, was a member of the old County Wexford family of Rathronan Castle. He was a cousin of the Sinn Fein and Gaelic League activist and historian Kathleen Browne. A distinguished graduate of Maynooth he had the unusual distinction of being appointed a professor in St. Peter's College four months before he was ordained at the age of 24. He was parish priest in St. Martin's, Piercestown, when consecrated bishop in 1884. He died unexpectedly following the June 1917 meeting of the Irish bishops in Maynooth.

Bishop William Codd was from a Wexford port seafaring family. His famed sea-captain uncle who reared him was known to terrify the fainthearted by refusing to lower a stitch of sail in a gale until the last possible moment. William Codd himself was an intrepid seaman "... few could handle the sails with greater dexterity. His daring was equal to his skill and many a time it was only his marked seamanship that enabled him to fight, always alone, against sudden storms and tempestuous seas". He was ordained in Rome where he was a student in the Irish College. On his return he was appointed professor of Dogmatic Theology in St. Peter's seminary. He became President of the college in 1903 and parish priest of seaside Blackwater in 1912. He was fluent in several European languages and had a special interest in geology, music and astronomy. He was consecrated bishop in February 1918. It is claimed that he moved the bishops residence from St. Mary's Summerhill to the present location because he could not bear being cut off from sight of the sea.

The funeral of Bishop James Browne moves through Enniscorthy. The Men's Confraternity is led by their own band. He died unexpectedly while on holidays in Malahide on the 17th June 1917.

Bishop Browne's successor, Dr. William Codd, at left, enters Wexford as his carriage reaches the top of Hill Street. The reason for the empty space is that horses and ponies had to make a faster pace going up a steep type of hill. Other horse-drawn vehicles allowed them their fair degree of space.

St. Peter's College students 1916. The posed photograph of the diocesan seminary lay-side students was taken in April, 1916 by Charles Vize. The students would have come from all parts of the diocese of Ferns. There is one unusual distinction. The names for the back row are given from right to left. The identities, by courtesy of the Diocesan Archivist, are written by hand as follows: Back row, right to left; J. O'Connor, M. Kennedy, P. Doyle, P. O'Connor, E. Doyle, M. Doran, T. Quigley, J. Murphy, M. Kinsella, J. O'(indecipherable), M. Kavanagh, J. Quigley, D.

The Right Rev. John Godfrey FitzMaurice Day. Church of Ireland Bishop of Ferns 1920-1938.

Doyle, "Embekay" (sic), R. Sutton, G. Bolger, M. Kinsella, N. Redmond. Notice the next line of boys is written as follows-Standing, left to right: F. Marshal, J. Roche, M. Sutton, J. Murphy (senr.) J. Murphy (jnr.) T. Roche, J. Doherty, J. Stafford, J. (indecipherable) M. Burns (or Burne), T. Power, G. Haden (sic), P. O'Brien, A. Mullins, J. Larkin, M. Burns (or Burne). Sitting, left to right: T. Pierce, B. Fitzsimons, T. Moran, J. Codd, T. Cullen, W. Fitzpatrick, L. McLoughlin, Rev. J. Carty, Rev. J. Donovan, B.D. (Dean), E. Kehoe, L. Webb, L. O'Gorman, J. Barry, D. Carton. Sitting (bottom row): E. Balfe, M. O'Leary, J. Dunne, F. Hearne, T. Lambert, F. Berry, T. Maghet (sic), P. Berry, B. O'Connor, G. Hearne and D. MacLoughlin! (as written). There are 57 students in the photograph, a relatively small number, one might think, if it comprises the entire student body. However when it is borne in mind that in the World War Two period, twenty five years later on, the numbers of lay students did not exceed 120, the figure for 1916 seems acceptable.

(Courtesy Canon Seamus de Vál)

Abbot Marmion (centre, with abbatial cross) and his community in Edermine House. *(Michael Fitzpatrick Collection)*

MONKS AT EDERMINE

After the occupation of south western Belgium by the German army at the beginning of the First World War in 1914, the Benedictine community in Maredsous were forced to seek refuge elsewhere. Dom Columba, the Abbot, a Dublin man, left Belgium disguised as a cattle jobber to seek a place where they could live. Failing to find any accommodation in England, he came to Ireland and succeeded in acquiring Edermine House at Edermine, Co. Wexford, the ancestral home of the Power family. The monks occupied Edermine on 21 November 1914, and on Christmas Day Dom Columba Marmion solemnly opened and blessed the new priory, and appointed Dom Aubert Merten as prior, with Dom Patrick Nolan as sub-prior. Dom Columba was extremely grateful to the Bishop of Ferns, Dr. James Browne, for his assistance in the whole operation, and wrote in Saint Peter's College Annual for 1916: *"The Belgian monks of Maredsous... found a home and a hearty welcome on their arrival in Wexford, when persecution and need obliged them to seek a temporary home in Ireland"*.

Dom Columba Marmion, Abbot of Maredsous, Belgium who with his Benedictive community found refuge in Edermine House.

The visit of Bishop James Browne to the Benedictine Community in Edemine, circa 1916. He was accompanied by his senior clergy and the Guardian of the Franciscan Friary in Wexford. Dom Marmion, the author of several spiritual books in French and English, became exceptionally influential and popular because of his infectious goodness. On the return to Belgium with his monks he continued to write and lecture. One collection of his homilies at conferences was published as recently as 1996. At the beginning of 1923 an epidemic of influenza swept through the abbey of Maredsous, and the abbot fell victim to the disease. He celebrated Mass for the last time on 25 January, the feast of the Conversion of St. Paul, and he died five days later. Dom Marmion was beatified by Pope John Paul II on 3 September, 2000. The layman at back, extreme right, is the active and influential solicitor, Michael J. O'Connor, Westlands. *(Michael Fitzpatrick Collection)*

Preceeded by crossbearer, acolytes and banner, a procession wends its way along a Wexford street. There is a flag flying from an upstairs window, a banner and two wreaths, while on the further away houses there are garlands. It appears like upper John Street, Wexford and the horse-drawn carriage or hearse follows. This Alice White photograph is not titled.

Drama claims the stage of St. Peter's College Seminary in 1917. Surprisingly (if you will), the play chosen (or allowed) was one of startling clerical controversy dealing with a priestly vocation imposed on a young man by his mother and father. The young author was the celebrated T. C. Murray. The play, "Maurice Harte" was premiered in the Abbey Theatre in 1912 and then performed in the Royal Court, London. Murray, as a national school teacher, had bitter experience of clerical school management. He died laden with academic honours in 1959. The cast of the play, standing: Morgan Walshe ("P. T. Mangan"), M. O'Carroll (the Maynooth student), P. Treacy ("Mrs. O'Connor"), Denis Doyle, Craanford, later P.P. Piercestown (Maurice Harte's brother) and M. Moore ("Michael Harte"). Seated: Nicholas Cardiff, Murrintown, later P.P. Ballyoughter ("Maurice Harte"), Tom Dunlea ("Mrs. Harte") and Thomas O'Brien ("Fr. Mangan"). *(Diocesan Archives)*

CHURCH AND CONSCRIPTION 1918

On 16 April 1918 the Conscription to include all Ireland Bill was passed in London. A meeting was convened in the Mansion House, Dublin, of politicians of all sides, parliamentarians and Sinn Fein, on 18 April, and an anti-conscription pledge drawn up (formulated by Eamon de Valera).

At that time the Irish Catholic hierarchy assembled in Maynooth for their annual meeting. A delegation from the Mansion House conference approached them and asked them to issue a statement, authorising or sanctioning resistance to the conscription. This was done without delay, the Bishops' manifesto declaring:

"We consider that conscription forced in this way upon Ireland is an oppressive and inhuman law which the Irish people have a right to resist by every means that are consonant with the law of God".

On Sunday, 21 April, a declaration against conscription was signed by the public all over the country in Irish as well as English.

THE CIVIL WAR 1922-23

The Civil War was well named in Irish, 'Cogadh na gCaraid', in English the "War of the Friends'. Following the truce there was a period of reflection, rest and political manoeuvres. A treaty between Ireland and Britain was discussed and negotiated in London. The negotiations were tortuous and ended with compromise. The final terms signed were greeted by many as the freedom to obtain freedom. Others regarded them with horror and while partition had already been copper-fastened, the acceptance of conditions like British Dominion status and an oath of allegiance to England's monarch was abhorrent and extremely so. In view, however, of the strategic importance of Ireland to Britain the achievement of the measure of freedom was a massive accomplishment.

The so-called Anglo-Irish Treaty was signed in London on 6 December, 1922. The Dáil controlled Irish Republican Army gradually split into two separate forces, the new Free State Army and the anti-Treaty Republican Army. General elections were called for June 1922 after which the Treaty with Britain was again endorsed by Dáil Éireann.

There were pogroms against nationalists in Ulster. Military activity was supported for a period by both sides of Sinn Féin, pro-Treaty and anti-Treaty, against the newly installed regime in Belfast. The Northern Ireland government called in as its adviser Field Marshal Sir Henry Wilson, Chief of the Imperial General staff, an advocate of the reconquest of Ireland by military force. He was assassinated by two Sinn Féin Volunteers, John O'Brien and James Connolly, on 22 June, 1922, in London. There was almost ungovernable fury in the Westminster House of Commons.

The Prime Minister, Lloyd George had exercised extreme pressure on the Free State government to break absolutely with the Republican forces if they intended to preserve the Treaty. He urged British military intervention. On June 22 the Free State army opened fire with field guns on the Four Courts in Dublin which had been occupied as headquarters by the anti-treaty Republican forces on 14 April, 1922. The leaders of those Republican forces included Rory O'Connor and Liam Mellows.

Ireland's "War of the Friends" had begun. The split between anti-treaty and pro-treaty adherents was country≤wide but Co. Wexford became one of the most violent counties in the Civil War. The conflict which scarred and divided families followed the pattern of guerrilla warfare. It was so viciously fought that veterans of the 1916 to 1921 struggle wondered why County Wexford, by comparison, had been so muted in the previous three years. At first the anti-treaty forces controlled all Wexford including Wexford town, Gorey and particularly Enniscorthy. They were dislodged by the Free State army, but groups waged continuous warfare against the newly-recruited soldiers, ambushing transports, hitting barracks, blowing up bridges, as at Taylorstown Bridge, or burning them as at the Redmond Bridge in Carcur. Retaliation killings, executions, murders, accompanied the military actions and military casualties as Wexford friends, families, along with sons and daughters, shared the nightmare of bitter mortal antagonisms.

The war on the railways by Republican forces was constant and heavy. As one veteran of the Civil War, Dr Peadar Sinnott explained, 'our aim was to make the Free State government impossible'. Reprisals followed attacks in a vicious circle. The killing of Free State soldiers was followed by the execution in Wexford Gaol of James Parle, Patrick Hogan and John Creane. Following the pattern, three Free State soldiers, Lieutenant T. Jones, Sergeant Edward O'Gorman and acting Sergeant Patrick Horan were captured in the Ballagh and executed in Adamstown. A senior Free State army officer, Commandant Peter Doyle, was shot in the grounds of Saint Aidan's Cathedral, Enniscorthy.

Two bishops of Ferns, Bishop James Browne (1884-1917), a native of Mayglass, and Bishop William Codd, a member of a noted sea-faring family (1917-1938), had presided over the diocese of Ferns in these years of turbulence. In October 1922 the bishops condemned the resistance to the provisional government in the following joint pastoral words, 'The guerilla warfare now being carried out by the Irregulars (anti-treaty forces) is without moral sanction and therefore the killing of national soldiers in the course of it is murder before God'. The condemnation had little effect and "the war of the friends" carried on.

When the Free State army billeted troops in the available larger houses they became targets. Soon the remains of burned mansions were added to the debris of war as bitterness increased. Four of the mansions destroyed were Wilton Castle, Castleboro, Ballinastraw and Bellevue in Ballyhogue. An ambush at Kyle on the main Wexford to Enniscorthy road resulted in fierce fighting. Four of the anti-treaty volunteers under Bob Lambert were killed and four men of the national army were wounded. For twelve months Irishmen fought Irishmen with unabated bitterness.

Flowers and markers at the spot in Ballybuick, Tomhaggard, where Commandant Michael Radford of the South Wexford Brigade, IRA, was shot and killed by Free State troops in June 1923.
(By courtesy of Paddy Berry)

On May 8, 1922, sides in the various sections and commands in Sinn Féin and in the Irish Republican Army had been taken. Hostilities between old War of Independence comrades were in imminent danger of escalation. A meeting to avert this civil war was arranged for the Mansion House, Dublin. On that day the IRA and newly formed National Army leaders met. Our photograph is one of several taken of the meeting. It is exceptional in that it gives a glimpse of these wartime colleagues in comradely, affable mood. The usual photographs show a contrasting grimness that is almost painful to study in view of the awful aftermath. The six are Seán MacEoin, Seán Moylan, Eoin O'Duffy, Liam Lynch, Gearóid O'Sullivan and Liam Mellows. (Sinnott Collection)

The IRA commandant, Dan Breen, with his friend in arms, General Seán McEoin, leaving the Sinn Féin Party Congress in Dublin's Mansion House on 22 February 1922. The gulf between pro-treaty and anti-treaty sides in Sinn Féin was growing wider. The conference of 3,000 delegates agreed to adjourn the convention for three months until the new Irish Free State constitution was placed before it.
(Courtesy late Dan Breen)

GOREY R.I.C. BARRACKS

the local dealers and as it clearly appears workmen are engaged in removing slates from Jackson's shop, to avoid burning that property. The workman is Tom Doyle, Garden City, Gorey. The Free State Army occupied St. Patrick's Club on Main Street and barricaded the building with sandbags. They later removed to the old workhouse buildings at Ramstown.

A leisurely pursuit, the demolition of an R.I.C. barracks involves no fuss, no hurry and but modest interest from spectators. The Republican arrangements carry on efficiently until the ultimate successful conclusion.

Following the Treaty members of the North Wexford Battalion of the IRA were in occupation of Gorey R.I.C. Barracks. As the Free State National Army moved towards the south east information about their intentions was transmitted to the IRA in Gorey. Preparations were immediately made to burn the R.I.C. Barracks and the Courthouse.

According to Gorey historian, Michael Fitzpatrick's informant, James Breen of Pearse Street, a man named Kinsella from Carnew was in charge of operations, and that he rode about on a motorcycle issuing commands.

Preparations had begun to burn the Courthouse and R.I.C. barracks and to blow up the Railway Bridge at Arklow Road to sever the rail connection from Dublin. The bridge at Corrigenagh is said to have been damaged to avert traffic from that direction. These photographs taken on the day 6th July 1922, depict the situation. Paddy Stokes, Main Street, Gorey was the custodian of wire used in the demolition of the Railway Bridge. Petrol for burning the civic buildings was taken from

The R.I.C. barracks in Gorey is prepared for destruction.

Gorey R.I.C. Barracks is in flames and the spectators gather as nonchalantly as if it were a lull in a football match.
(Michael Fitzpatrick Collection)

The burnt out R.I.C. barracks, Gorey. *(Michael Fitzpatrick Collection)*

Gorey Courthouse
in flames, 1922

This remarkable photo was taken at the
exact moment of the explosion at Gorey's
railway bridge, Arklow Road.
(Michael FitzPatrick Collection).

Aftermath of the explosion,
destruction and a halted train.

Republican soldiers leaving Gorey after demolishing the R.I.C. barracks and civic buildings.
(Michael Fitzpatrick Collection)

Suttons of Coole 1918. Back row: Tim and Annie. Front: Brigid, Thomas, Michael (in petticoat), Thomas, Kathleen, Margaret, Mary Ann, Richard. Inset: Johnny. Thomas Sutton lived in Ballykelly, married Margaret Brown of Coole. They had sixteen children, ten survived into adulthood. Thomas, known as "The Boss", was a quarter master with the I.R.A. and was captured early in the Civil War by Free State troops and interned in Wexford Jail.

(Fitzpatrick Collection)

Wexford bridge at Carcur wrecked and burned by republicans. *(Photo Alice White)*

Civil War. Volunteers of the Republican Army, anti-Treaty Forces, stand guard at their Wexford town H.Q., The Mechanics Institute, North Main Street, before Wexford's occupation by Free State troops. The sentry at right is Thomas Rossiter of Barrack Street, Wexford.

(Alice White Collection)

War on Wexford's Railways 1922-23

The comprehensive account of the Civil War attacks on the south east's communications has been brilliantly, and without offence, recorded in Dr. George Hadden's "The War on Wexford Railways 1922-1923" in The Journal of the Irish Railway Record Society, Vol. 3, 1952-54.

It has been complemented by another splendid account compiled by Dr. Christine Forde, Faculty of Education, University of Strathclyde, Scotland for her family as a tribute to her grandfather, Michael Forde, Inspector of Railways. We are deeply grateful to both for their work and their photographs. We are greatly indebted to author and railway historian Ernie Shepherd of Blackwater and John Walker of Glenbrook for their technical assistance and photos. If there are technical errors in the captions we do insist that it is not their fault.

This writer was present as a vocational schools student on the remarkable night George Hadden read his classic paper to the Old Wexford Society. It took place in the Wexford County Council's chambers before a pitifully small attendance of less than 30. However, that attendance included participants of major consequence in that civil war and in subsequent public life. They were Dr. Peadar "Pax" Sinnott, T. D. Sinnott, Co. Manager; Alderman Michael Flusk and the voluble engine driver, "Sketch" White. Even as theatre it was an unforgettable occasion.

The framework of the paper was built up on the well-documented recollections of Michael Forde, Permanent Way Inspector of the D. & S.E.R. in the Wexford area. To his loyalty, courage, initiative, resource and energy was due the continued running of the railway throughout the storm. His epitaph was spoken by one of his most indefatigable antagonists, and most devoted admirers, Dr. Peader Sinnott: "Old Forde", he said, "was a genius. And he adored his old railway." Dr. Sinnott himself and Michael Flusk – leaders both – have supplied the reverse side of the story. Their influence is felt on almost every page. Sketch White–engine driver, insurgent, and restless spirit–moves vividly through most of the narrative. Finally, T. D. Sinnott, brigadier during the Anglo-Irish War and during the Civil War, a very much perturbed neutral with many friends on both sides, supplied invaluable criticism, wise comment, and at least one deliciously revealing sidelight.

The nominal direction of the war on the railways lay with the Republican higher command, but it is doubtful whether during the Civil War it was ever in effective control of field operations. On the other hand it did issue general directives: to interrupt the railways by every possible means; to destroy rolling stock, or to ensure that stone houses capable of being fortified, should not fall into the hands of the Free State military. These orders were transmitted through the divisional adjutant. Divisional H.Q. for the south-east was at Dunmain. The orders were discussed by a brigade council meeting at some such central spot as Palace House or Taghmon, which, using women couriers, relayed them to section leaders "in the hope," so said Dr. Sinnott, "that something would happen". "Thereafter," he added, "everything was left to the enterprise,

skill, ingenuity and will-to-fight of the individual areas." "In practice," Sketch White commented, "each column acted on its own initiative. To that extent they were responsible to nobody." And that explains why activities were so sporadic. They were confined to areas occupied by small bands.

In the field the old insurgent companies were condensed into flying columns whose sections–North Wexford (Enniscorthy), South (Murrintown), Central Wexford (Kyle) and West (New Ross)–consisted of a dozen or a score of men recruited from the officers of the Old I.R.A. When a man joined a column he dedicated his life to the war. He became a marked man. There was no going back. "Once I left home," said Michael Flusk, simply, "I never saw it again till all was over."

Michael Flusk, elected Mayor of Wexford in 1951.

Killurin Railway Station as a quiet rural venue before war changed everything.
(*Tykillen Archives*)

INSPECTOR MICHAEL FORDE'S CAMPAIGN

At Killurin, six miles above Wexford, the railway station was perched where the Carrigmannan ridge abuts into the river in rocky cliffs. The embankment merges with the shoulder of the hills, walled like a little fort commanding both river and glen. In 1921 this was made a one-man station. "It was" said Sketch White (engine driver), "in every way a handy place for an ambush." As a station it had all the necessary features for stopping trains. It stood isolated on its hills. A single armed man could - and did – occupy it effectively; and a small band on the rising ground behind its wonderfully good cover of fences and little woods could dominate the embankment.

For miles below the station the line skirts the river, almost as if made for wrecking and again as Sketch notes there were plenty of little laneways and odd forgotten roads for escape and most importantly the people were 'friendly'. It was no coincidence that the most active band of raiders in the county was the Kyle Column, Kyle Cross being a mile and a half across the Slaney from Killurin and the leader of this column had grown up in Killurin.

On July 10th raiders blew up Bridge 399, 195 yards on the Wexford side of Killurin station–a 10ft. brick arch span carrying the line over the little lane leading down to Killurin Quay. The bridge was broken without warning, the signals set at clear to an oncoming train, and the crew were left to take their chance. In charity, this may have been due to inexperience. The train was the 4.15 a.m. Wexford to Waterford goods. The engine was No 17 (0-6-0), the driver, Mick Conway and his fireman, Thomas Lee. The rails were broken about 20ft. short of the wrecked bridge; but in some extraordinary fashion, the engine, which was travelling pretty fast, contrived to jump the gap. Conway was steaming her at the time, which may have helped her to clamber onto the sleepers at the far side. She took her tender with her and came to rest at right angles to the road, about her own length beyond the gap and lying completely outside the rails, on the landward side, with her left leading wheel overhanging the bank. The first wagon behind the tender failed to make the jump and fell, stern first, into the gap. But the coupling held, and by anchoring the engine it may just have saved her toppling down the bank. Had she gone down, the crew could scarcely have escaped with their lives. It was a close thing.

Word was telephoned through to Wexford about 5 a.m. At 7.30 the breakdown gang arrived at Killurin. Their first job was to secure the engine by building up a crib of sleepers under the overhanging wheel. Then, leaving the engine to Michael Cross, foreman of the Loco Department, Inspector Forde tackled the derailed wagons. He broke the tracks some distance behind the wreck and relaid it with flange rails out towards the scattered wagons. Then, with the aid of a long chain, the breakdown engine pulled the wagons one by one back onto the line. The one hanging in the gap they jacked up from below. That done, the gang made good the gap with an emergency bridge of timber baulks, laid a pair of rails under the jacked-up engine, broke the road again and pulled it over to join up with the engine rails. Then the breakdown engine hauled No. 17 back onto the main line. By 10.30 p.m. the line was clear for traffic.

Inspector Michael Forde faces the camera held in Tykillen Walker hands with wreckage on every side of him.
(Tykillen Archives)

No. 17, called "the Wicklow", at the north Railway Station, Wexford, in her prime. She was a war veteran in County Wexford having been derailed twice at least in the Civil War. She was built in 1899 and survived until scrapped in 1929. The date of the photograph is uncertain but it is believed that its eventual driver, "Sketch" White, is included, even though he cannot be pinpointed with certainty. He facilitated those he considered to be nationalist activists at all times. He frequently gave accounts of his wartime activities on the railways, allotting to himself heroic if amusing roles. He made many oral contributions to the Wexford Historical Society of which he was a member.

KILLURIN AMBUSH

At 4.30 on July 24, 1922, when Philip Fox, the Killurin station master, came on to the platform, as was his custom, to watch the Wexford Mail go through at speed, he saw 10 to 12 armed men running towards him. While the rest ran on, one stayed behind to attend to the station. He forced Fox to put the signals at danger. Then he demanded the red flag, locked Fox into his office, threw the key there and went to fix the flag between the rails 100 yards outside the station.

Half an hour earlier, in Wexford, 40 prisoners were put on board the train under an escort of 46 men. The escort – Lieut. P. Leonard in charge – occupied the first and third coaches, the prisoners the second. In the rear coach were 25 unarmed recruits under Capt. Myles Redmond. The rest of the train was crowded in every compartment by ordinary passengers. That day the guard did not report for duty. He sent word that "he'd sprained his ankle." Sketch White was on the engine and with him on the footplate was Inspector Forde. T. D. Sinnott was to travel from Wexford by that train. At the station he joined up with a friend – "a worthy citizen of Enniscorthy" – also travelling.

They had just taken their tickets when the station master approached T. D. Sinnott privately and said in a very low voice, "You're not to travel on this train". "Why?, What's wrong with it?" "There's nothing wrong with it." "Then why am I not to travel on it?" "I was told to tell you and that ought to be good enough for you." It was. He turned to his associate and said "How about a drink across at the Imperial while we're waiting?" "But have we time?" "Lots of time – and anyhow they'll hold her a few minutes for me." So off they went and off went the train without them – to no small vexation of the good citizen. But for ever after, when they met again, he'd say "Wasn't it the lucky thing we missed that train!"

The train started on time. After passing Killurin Tunnel she slowed down for the temporary bridge – No. 399 – outside the station. Just as she overran the red flag the firing started from the rising ground outside the station. A hundred yards further, the engine being just within the cover of the 8ft. brick wall of the station, and the rest of the train strung out in the open on the embankment, they stopped with all brakes on, Sketch shouting across the engine that there was a rail dislodged ahead. The firing was coming from behind a hedge at about

Left: Captain N. Clarke (Dublin), Right: Lieutenant Leonard. Centre: Myles Redmond, Wexford. Captain 41st Battalion, 3rd Eastern Division, National Army. Taken August 21, 1922

(Myles Redmond Jr. Collection)

15 yards. Fire was concentrated on the first and third coaches. The escort clambered down on the permanent way and sheltering behind the wheels, returned the fire. The prisoners were lying on the floor of the second coach and praying to be let out. The captain of the escort came up to the engine and ordered White to draw the train on into the shelter of the station wall. White said his brakes were jammed. Meanwhile, Forde ran up the platform looking for the station master. He found the key and released him. Then he telephoned to Wexford and Enniscorthy that the mail was being ambushed and to send ambulances for three badly wounded men. All three died. Meanwhile, the military had occupied the station and were developing a dangerous encircling movement to take the ambush in the rear. So the raiders, having failed to panic the escort or to rescue the prisoners, withdrew, and about 25 minutes after the first shots, firing ceased.

When the train moved on, a couple of army officers rode on the engine. There proved to be nothing wrong with the brakes or with the tracks. A mile beyond the station they came upon a "pump bogie" left on the line by the raiders after they had taken off its crew of linesmen returning from an inspection. At Macmine, an hour behind time, the 4.15 from Enniscorthy was waiting on the down line, Mike Hogan on the engine. All agog for the latest news –for he was due to take his train through Killurin 15 minutes later – he ran round to have a talk with Sketch on the mail engine. But he never reached her. The running boards of the leading coaches were a horror of blood oozing out from under the doors. He went no farther. He thought he would never get back to his own engine to be sick. But when he reached Killurin he found all quiet.

At Enniscorthy, Sketch White was taken off his engine and arrested for being in collusion with the ambush and so responsible for the death of the three soldiers. It was then he was assaulted by Jem Doyle (who was later shot by the raider himself) because the three dead men had been his comrades. White was put into the second coach with the other prisoners. The coaches were detached from the mail which, now being two hours late, was sent on immediately while the three military coaches were made up as a special through to Harcourt St. The train went on with the driver and firemen fearful of further attacks. They were right to be nervous, a wrecking party from Dalkey missed them only by minutes. However, all was still not safe. At Harcourt St., in the station itself, the train was ambushed for a second time though again unsuccessfully. The prisoners were then taken off to jail with Sketch White among them. He was released six weeks later but arrested again the following February and held until October 1923.

Train driver "Sketch" White.

Killurin goods train derailment.

Michael Forde's rail relaying gang take a spell from urgent work for the cameraman.

KILLURIN TUNNEL

Just over two weeks after the ambush at Killurin station, Killurin was yet again the site of further trouble which involved Inspector Forde. On 15th August 1922 two lengths of rail were removed from within the Wexford end of the Killurin tunnel. Again there was no warning and the down night mail, a goods train ran into the trap. The engine left the rails but continued to run on the ground for about 150 yards till she went onto soft ground and turned over. The engine driver, George Turner, was pinned in the engine.

Word was received in Wexford at 5.20am that Turner was missing. Inspector Forde immediately telephoned the military for an ambulance. It arrived in 15 minutes and Forde himself guided it to Killurin where they got Turner out, badly scalded but alive. He was off work for a year but did make a good recovery.

The breakdown train arrived about 7.15am. All day long Forde worked on the wagons – 22 of them – mostly coal. He sent up to Edermine for a load of flange rails. With these he got the wagons back on to the road, sending each up to

Dr. George Hadden, author of "The War on the Wexford Railways 1922-27," in The Journal of the Irish Railway Record Society.

Macmine sidings while the gang lengthened the temporary rails for the next coach and then eventually the train.

On this occasion Forde did not have to deal with gunshot but instead locals pilfering from the train. Hadden quotes Inspector Forde: "They were demoralised and the amount of pilfering was disgraceful. You couldn't watch 'em. They'd take anything. They came with horses and carts from far and near. Besides, the coal, there was a consignment of tea on that train and £300 worth of drapery goods. For long afterwards there was all the tea the countryside could use." He knew of one house in the area that had 35 velour hats. But Forde had to contend with the more difficult task of keeping the line open.

"Property should not be the concern of the breakdown gang, yet most of the time there was only myself there. I had my own work to do; but if the senior officials of the company were disinclined to venture near a wreck – and that was notorious – I did my best. At least I collected up all the parcels and moveable property and got it off safely." [Since I have many friends in the Killurin Macmine area I would not be prepared to make further comment. *Nicholas Furlong*]

That day by 10 pm Forde and the breakdown gang had the wagons back on the rails, but the Loco Dept were struggling to right the engine. Finally, an endless chain block was brought from Thompsons on the Quay and they were able to get the engine on its wheels and by 2 a.m they had the rails under her. Then they relaid the main line in a curve around her to let through the night goods from Wexford. The next day, after another train had gone through to Dublin, the Gang returned. They broke the tracks and joined them up under the wrecked train and pulled it onto the main line to be towed back to Wexford. Then the line was relaid.

No. 14 collapsed after the
Killurin Tunnel trap.
(Courtesy of Ernest Shepherd)

Michael Forde, at left
in bowler hat, bearing
the authority of a
shining watch chain,
poses with his steam
engine and officials in
the wreckage at
Macmine Junction. The
photograph could
represent many days
between 1922 and
1923.

Michael Forde and his men rebuild the temporary signals and cabin at Enniscorthy following the IRA demolition and burning on September 16th 1922

Breakdown gang at Killurin. A railway official is also present. There is a supporting engine at the rear. The previous evening two lengths of rail had been ripped up. The night mail train was derailed. It took two days to restore normal service, if indeed the word normal is appropriate.

One of Michael Forde's gangers checking every foot of rail on an inspection bicycle near Macmine Junction

Repairing the signal box at the vital link with Waterford and Ross, Macmine Junction. At the time Macmine was in such travelled use for New Ross, Waterford, Cork and midlands traffic that major manufacturers like Tylers and Bovril had permanent advertisements installed on the platform.

The isolation of Waterford. The destruction of Taylorstown Viaduct and of Bridge 457 were associated with the opening phases of the Civil War when the I.R.A. was trying to isolate Waterford from attack. Both were simple operations. The historic barrier of Waterford follows the line of the Barrow from the mountains to the sea, and both its great railway bridges are vulnerable. But demolition of those steel-girder spans called for more high explosive and skilled technique than the raiders may have had at their command just then. Nor, indeed, could they easily have improved on the results actually attained at Taylorstown. The Taylorstown Viaduct carries the South Wexford line over the Owenduff River near Wellington Bridge. It was built of brick and when one day early in July the raiders blew up one arch, three others collapsed like a house of cards. The line was out of commission for the duration and for long afterwards. The Cork-Rosslare expresses were still being worked round by Macmine up to Christmas the following year.

FORDE'S GREATEST CHALLENGE

On 11th November, outside Killurin station, the rails were pulled out of the edge of the embankment and broken just before the arrival of the night goods from Dublin with Engine No. 18 again. This time the raiders stopped the train by signal and took off the crew before wrecking the engine.

No. 18 was a powerful engine, built in the Company's own works. She rolled down the bank at Killurin like a boulder, rolling over and over. The marks of her were on the bank but the damage to the engine was minimal. The engine had finally ended up on its side in the Slaney river, just below Killurin Quay.

The engine was sunk about half way in the mud. At high tide she was completely under water. Only for two hours at low tide could the gang work at her,

Inspector Michael Forde

and then deep in mud. Their first job was to get her on her wheels. To do that they had to provide a solid platform from which to operate their lifting jacks. This they contrived in the form of a crib of sleepers built out in the river.

It was a long job and in the course of it Forde and the breakdown gang used the extra services of many a passing engine for as long as she could be spared from her train.

The scene at Killurin, below and at left bottom of opposite page, when the No. 18 was derailed and ended up in the river.

Heavy Free State army presence alongside a derailed
engine near Killurin. Michael Forde is at left forground.

Free State army reinforcements at Killurin Station. the armed men standing at the engines front buffers are
Sean O'Kennedy, New Ross (at left), Myles Redmond, Wexford (at right). *(Myles Redmond Collection)*

SPARROWSLAND

Sparrowsland siding is an isolated siding at the base of the wooded heights of Bree Hill. On the evening of 20th November 1922, raiders held up the Waterford goods there, on its way to connect at Macmine with the main-line goods. They stopped her by lamps and fog signals, "wherever they got hold of them," remarked Inspector Forde. The raiders ran the train a mile east of the siding to a little clear running river where they broke the line, pulled the rails to the edge of the bank and having unhooked Engine No. 36 ran her into the marsh. They had left the wagons back at the siding.

About 10.30 p.m. Macmine reported to Wexford that the Waterford goods was taken. Inspector Forde came on duty and made all the arrangements for the breakdown train to get off after first Mass in the morning. She ran with staff to Macmine and there took the pilot porter for the last three miles to Sparrowsland. They found the engine lying face down in the soft ground at the edge of the low bank. The rails were twisted so that meant finding and fetching new rails – a time-wasting job. Nevertheless, by evening they had made good the line and got the wagons to Macmine for distribution. The salving of the engine took a week. "To the men who got the No. 18 and No. 32 out of the Slaney there was no serious difficulty in building a track under her from here" commented Inspector Forde, but this was thought unnecessary because there was no tide and so they decided to dismantle the engine where she lay and as they brought up each large part they transported it to the siding where the whole engine could be reassembled again.

D. & S.E.R. No. 36
derailed near
Sparrowsland

Palace East

Palace East was a very sleepy junction but for all its seeming quietness, Dr. Hadden suggests in his published work *War on the Railways* that "that nest of mountain boundaries around Polmonty Pass is one of the wildest areas in Ireland. Three counties converge there ... and such mountainy borderlands have at all times been sanctuaries for outlaws, and if there is anything in heredity, these mountainy people may well even now take a poor view of Governments in general". Inspector Forde certainly thought so, and he may perhaps be forgiven a touch of asperity in his references to them. Sardonically surveying this nest of troubles he said: 'These mountainy folk were an awful law-breaking crowd. Out for loot and what they could get out of the troubles. When they held up a train they took everything but the engine." [These characteristics no longer obtain in the region–*Nicholas Furlong*]. But Inspector Forde was also emphatic in his opinion that the root of the trouble on both sides of New Ross lay in disloyalty amongst the company's own staff. Though what the Inspector did not know was that Palace House was the centre of operations in the whole insurgents' campaign and a meeting place for the Brigade Council. The signal cabin at Palace East was attacked on 15th September 1922.

Palace East bridge cut by anti-treaty troops, referred to as the IRA or alternatively "Irregulars" by the Free State army and government.

DOGS ROAD BRIDGE

At the end of February 1923 Inspector Forde came back to deal with a wreck at Dogs Road Bridge. He had a ballast train with a load of rails. It was Sunday and he reckoned to have the line to himself. But, though the major guerrilla operations against the railway had ended with the Palace East wreck of February 23rd, minor operations were keeping the wires cut everywhere and the roads unsafe. A party of raiders had somehow captured a train outside Waterford and had been running men into the New Ross area. It so happened that they got off the road before the ballast train went through or there'd have been trouble for everybody.

Once arrived at Dog's Road Bridge the breakdown gang got to work; but they weren't long at it when a party of armed raiders were seen coming. The raiders explained they had only come to collect revolvers which they had concealed in the tender. So the raiders collected them and left the gang to deal with the No. 39 in the same way they had dealt with the No. 17 at Ballyanne; they got rails under her and towed her till they got her back on the rails. Then they towed her to Wexford and thence to Dublin. As for the coaches they had disappeared completely during the month: there was nothing left but the wheels!

Re-railing No. 39 at Dog's
Road Bridge.
(Courtesy of Ernest Shepherd)

THE BALLYANNE
COLLISION

On 10th January 1923 Ganger Carton wired Inspector Forde: *"Something has gone wrong with Engine 25 gone through New Ross no tender."*
Later he wired again:
"No.56 and tender No. 25 derailed in collision Ballyanne Bank."

Following these two telegrams, came a third from O'Brien, Station Master at New Ross:
"To Inspector Forde, Murphy (Traffic Manager), Cross (Loco, Foreman) Wexford: No 56 engine and carriages derailed Ballyanne. Van and No 26 wagons pigs at Rathgarogue. No. 25 gone through New Ross no tender nor no man. What about 26 wagons of pigs? Can anything be done."

Darkness was falling when the raiders held up the train at Rathgarogue. They unhooked the pigs and left them there. Then, leaving No. 56 and the No. 2 coaches ready to follow on, they took No. 25 out through Ballintubber cutting onto the Ballyanne bank, to stage a run back collision. The driver, Michael Hogan, was made to run the train back to the Ballyanne bank, threatened at gun point to stop the train the minute the raider said so. This was a difficult task because the steam brake with all the stopping and starting was slow to respond. However, things got even stickier for all those on the No 25. Something went wrong with the timing. The plan had been to collide the No. 25 with the No. 56. As the No. 25 stopped, Peadar Sinnott, one of the raiders, happened to glance behind him. Rushing upon him through the darkness, breathing smoke and flame came No. 56, driverless, with open throttle and fully advanced slide valves. Steam glowing red with blazing sparks shot through the funnel. Hogan and Lee (the fireman) disappeared off the footplate, and Sinnott "with the instinct to run" leaped for the regulator and pulled it wide open. Then he jumped "bolting down the bank like a shot rabbit just as the avenging demon hit No. 25".

The impact of the No. 56 sent the No. 25 roaring off down the rail to New Ross and stopped a few miles out towards Glenmore. The No. 56 on impact, using the wrecked tender of the No. 25, charged down the line tearing up the road and causing widespread damage. This was a terrifying experience for railway men and raiders alike. Hogan, the engine driver, later recalled: "I got out of her with a few seconds to spare and it added 10 years to my age!

Dr. Peadar Sinnott, recorded his feelings: "I've been in some tight corners, but that was the worst. The crash came as I was going down the bank, and I remember, when I was picking myself up out of the fence at the bottom, hearing something heavy–a buffer, perhaps–plunge into the field a 100 yards away. I never asked how the No. 25 got started. Panic perhaps. I'd left a good man in charge; and so long as we achieved the essence of the main plan I never bothered the men about details that may have gone astray."

Next morning breakdown's first problem was to get through to the point of the obstruction. There were 26 wagons of pigs at Rathgarogue that first needed to be moved and then they got through. There they found the road ploughed up over a distance of 100 yards but by 4.30pm the twisted rail was replaced and the pig-train sent through to Waterford much to the relief of the Station Master.

No. 17 on the way down
the Ballyanne Bank with
apparently posing
spectators.
(Courtesy of Ernest Shepherd)

No. 17 back on make
shift rails under the
Ballyanne Railway
bank.
(Courtesy Ernest Shepherd)

Another day's work at Killurin.

Engine of the J20 class, pulling a mixed train, made an almost total wreck at Ballyanne on October 15th 1922.

THE ENGINE THAT STEAMED ON THE ROAD

On January 16th 1923 at Rathgarogue the so-called "raiders" held up the five o'clock mixed train from Macmine. It consisted of an engine No. 17 (0-6-0), one six wheel coach and 10 wagons of cattle. The cattle wagons were unhooked and left at the platform; the engine and the coach were taken out to Ballyanne bank, where over Ballyanne Old Bridge, they had broken the road and pulled it to the edge of a 76-foot escarpment. There they sent the engine over, with her coach and she capsized but lay where she fell. The coach remained on the rails. It was in this state of affairs that breakdown found the train. The first task of the breakdown gang was to get the coach back to Palace East. The next job was not so easy.

The engine was lying head down, at an angle of 45 degrees, just below the edge of the bank, with her tender still fouling the rails. The crew was unsure what would happen if they disturbed the engine in this precarious position. They re-routed some rails to take care of the tender and then set to work on the No. 17. The first step was to lay sleepers down the bank before her, and then, with Thompson's endless-chain block hooked to a tree below, they slewed her round and slid her on her side head – first to the toe of the bank. There they jacked her onto her wheels and laid rails under her, got steam on her and ran her on the county road. Here they only had six pairs of flange rails and no sleepers so the rails were laid with the gauge held by tiebars and the engine began to creep along. As she cleared one pair of rails, they were detached and rushed round ahead to be bolted in position ready for the engine as she moved slowly along. About a mile ahead the county road ran level with the railway tracks and here they cut in on the line and ran the engine back on to the railway, eventually bringing her into Wexford under her own steam. "Powerful strength these engines have," said Michael Forde, "except when they meet anything hard like themselves. Just get them back on the rails and work them away!"

Sketch White himself mourned the grand engines that were destroyed, among them his own engine, No. 68. The two new super-heater goods engines Nos. 15 and 16 were then due for delivery and it was the reaction against the destruction of No. 68 that made Sketch say one day to Sir Thomas Esmonde, then chairman of the D. & S.E.R., "I'd advise you to keep them engines out of here for fear they'd do them a mischief." Sir Thomas Esmonde conveyed the warning to the Board, and the two engines were sent to Belfast and stored by the G.N.R. in Adelaide Shed for the duration. "I shouldn't have done it," said Sketch "but I couldn't help it."

Re-railing No. 39 at Dog's
Road Bridge
*(Courtesy of Ernest Shepherd
and Irish Railway Record
Society)*

No. 17 helpless after the
Ballyanne Bank
demolition. *(Courtesy of
Ernest Shepherd and Irish
Railway Record Society)*

KILLINGS NEAR PALACE EAST

In relation to the deaths on 24 March 1923 of Lt. Thomas Jones, Sgt. Patrick Gorman and A/Sgt Patrick Horan, members of the 47th Battalion, Kilkenny Military Barracks, Waterford Command and attached at the time to the 41st Battalion Wexford Barracks for duty at Palace East, Co. Wexford, we have been given the following details. The two Sergeants were veterans of the British Army (Royal Irish Regiment) and had served throughout the Great War. They had enlisted at Kilkenny Barracks some few days before their deaths and were not yet issued with National Army uniform at the time of their murder by Irregulars. Lt. Jones had been appointed to commissioned rank by the then Col. Prout, OC Waterford Command. Jones had served from 1918 to 1922 as a Squad Leader, with "K" Company, 3rd Dublin Battalion, IRA and had been active in the Pearse Street area of Dublin city.

```
COPY.                              H.Q.41st Battn.
                                     Military Barracks,
   Ref.C.W.1/148.                      Wexford.
                                        25/3/23.


   TO,
      Command I. O.
         Borstal Barracks,
            CLONMEL.


   PALACE EAST-  At 2p.m. on Friday the 23rd inst. Vol. Keane,
                 Sgt. O'Gorman and Pte. Horan left Palace East
                 Post without permission.  They proceeded to a
                 publichouse two miles distant from the post.
                 At 8 p.m. the O.C, Palace East received a report
                 that these three soldiers were creating a
                 disturbance at the publichouse.  Lieut. Jones
                 and Vol. Croke proceeded to investigate the
                 case armed with revolvers.  On entering the
                 publichouse they were immediately surrounded by
                 a large party of Irregulars armed with rifles
                 and Thompson Guns.  Vol. Croke attempted to
                 draw his revolver and was fired on being wounded
                 in the hip.  Lt. Jones Segt. O'Gorman  and
                 Pte. Horan were taken to Adamstown.  A local
                 priest was made attend them and afterwards
                 each soldier was perforated with bullets from
                 a Thompson gun.  Their legs and bodies were a
                 mass of bullet marks.  Immediately work reached
                 Wexford Barracks, an Ambulance and Troops were
                 despatched to the scene.  Vol. Croke who was
                 badly wounded was brought to hospital in
                 New Ross.  The three dead bodies were found
                 in an outhouse near Adamstown and were brought
                 to Wexford Barracks.  The names of the three
                 men are:-
                     Lt. Thos. Jones, 50 Pleasant St. off Camden
                         St., Dublin.
                     Vol. Patrick Horan, Callan, Co. Kilkenny.
                     Sgt. Edward O"Gorman, Wellington Place,
                         Kilkenny.
```

                                                    (Sgd).

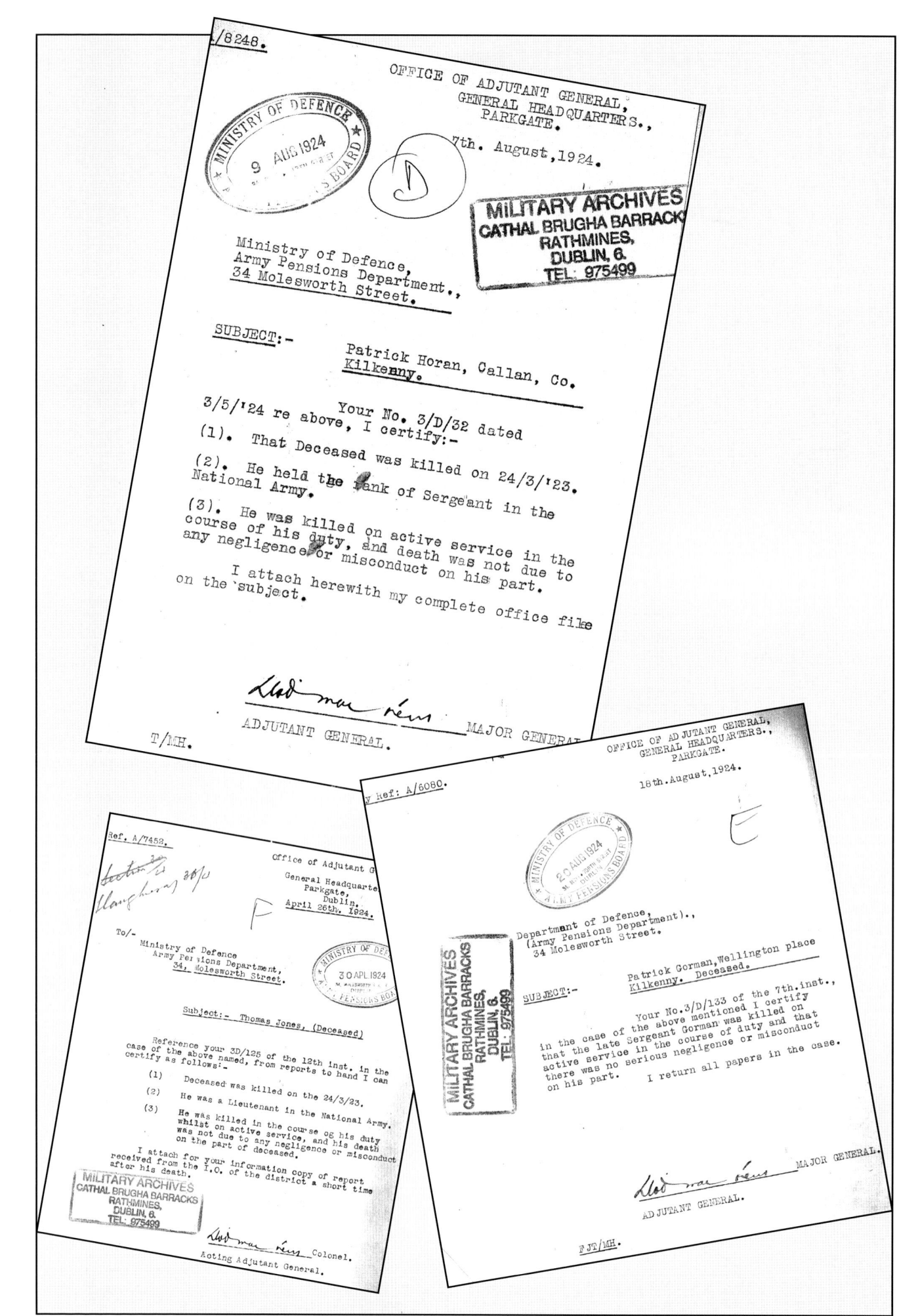

OFFICE OF ADJUTANT GENERAL.,
GENERAL HEADQUARTERS.,
PARKGATE.

/8248.

7th. August, 1924.

Ministry of Defence,
Army Pensions Department.,
34 Molesworth Street.

SUBJECT:-

Patrick Horan, Callan, Co.
Kilkenny.

Your No. 3/D/32 dated
3/5/'24 re above, I certify:-

(1). That Deceased was killed on 24/3/'23.

(2). He held the rank of Sergeant in the
National Army.

(3). He was killed on active service in the
course of his duty, and death was not due to
any negligence or misconduct on his part.

I attach herewith my complete office file
on the subject.

MAJOR GENERAL
ADJUTANT GENERAL.

T/MH.

Ref. A/7452.

Office of Adjutant G
General Headquarte
Parkgate,
Dublin,
April 26th. 1924.

To:- Ministry of Defence
Army Pensions Department,
34, Molesworth Street.

Subject:- Thomas Jones, (Deceased)

Reference your 3D/125 of the 12th inst. in the
case of the above named, from reports to hand I can
certify as follows:-

(1)   Deceased was killed on the 24/3/23.

(2)   He was a Lieutenant in the National Army.

(3)   He was killed in the course of his duty
whilst on active service, and his death
was not due to any negligence or misconduct
on the part of deceased.

I attach for your information copy of report
received from the I.O. of the district a short time
after his death.

Colonel.
Acting Adjutant General.

OFFICE OF ADJUTANT GENERAL,
GENERAL HEADQUARTERS.,
PARKGATE.

Ref: A/6080.

18th. August, 1924.

Department of Defence,
(Army Pensions Department).,
34 Molesworth Street.

SUBJECT:-

Patrick Gorman, Wellington place
Kilkenny. Deceased.

Your No. 3/D/133 of the 7th. inst.,
in the case of the above mentioned I certify
that the late Sergeant Gorman was killed on
active service in the course of duty and that
there was no serious negligence or misconduct
on his part.

I return all papers in the case.

MAJOR GENERAL.
ADJUTANT GENERAL.

FJT/MH.

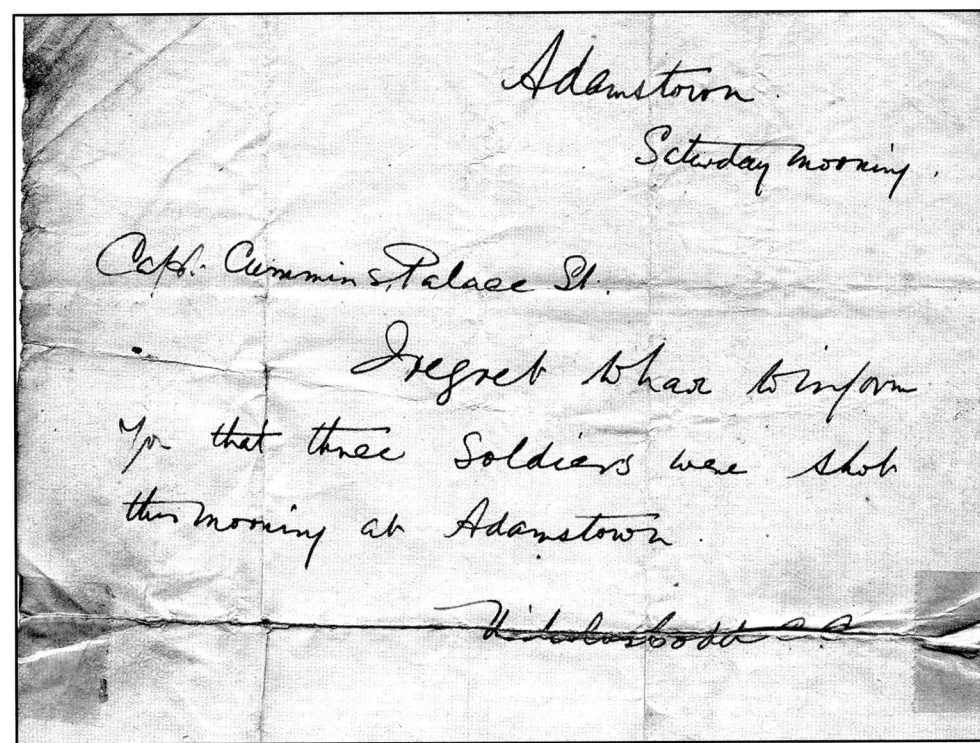

The curate in Adamstown, Fr. Michael Codd, informs the military of the execution of the three Free State soldiers. *(Sinnott Collection)*

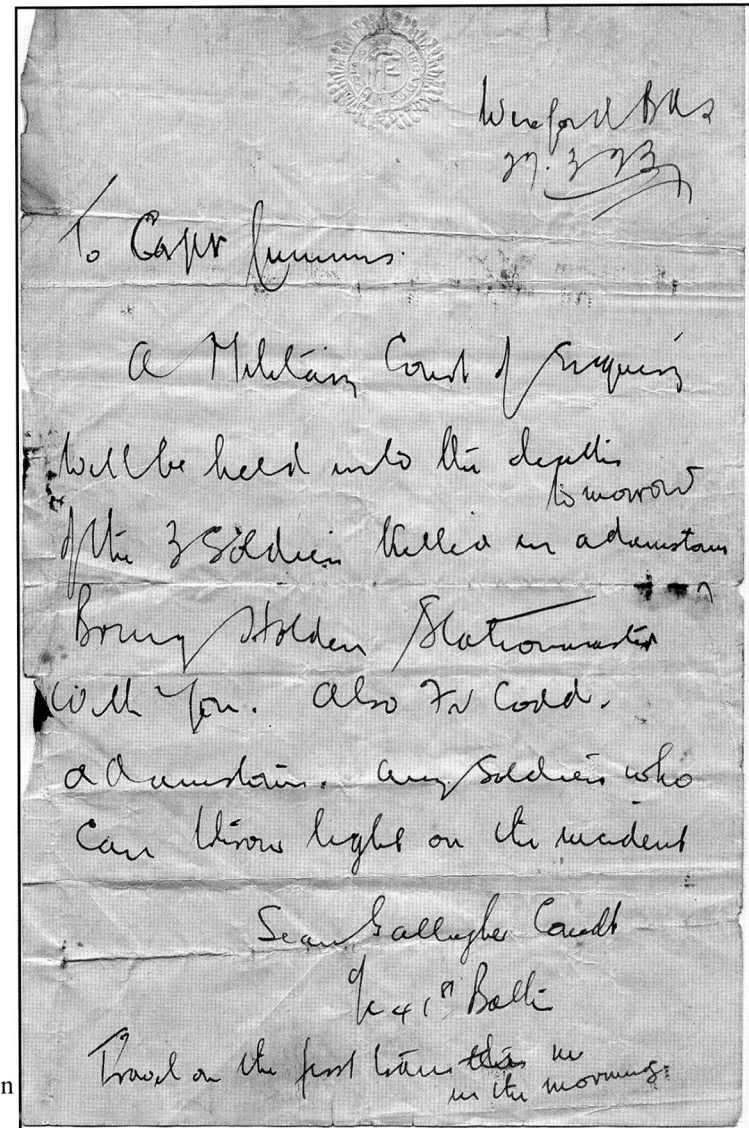

Military court of inquiry into the reprisal execution of the three Free State soldiers. *(Sinnott Collection)*

Statement by No. 18892 - Private JOHN CROKE H.Q.
Company, 20th Battalion, Gorey, in the case of
PATRICK HORAN (Deceased).

On the 23rd March 1923, I was one
of a detachment from Kilkenny station at Palace
East, Co. Wexford. The deceased was also
stationed there. Captain Cummins, now demobilised,
was in charge of the Post.

On the date in question, in consequence
of a complaint made to Captain Cummins ~ ̶ ̶ ̶ ·
 ̶ ̶ ̶ I was detailed to accompany Lieut. Jones
(who was attached to the Garrsion) to investigate
the complaint. We proceeded to McCabes Public House
about a mile from the town, and were in course
hearing the details of the case in the kitchen of
the house, when Sergt. Gorman and Volunteer Horan
(Deceased) entered. This was about 8.55 p.m. as
far as I can remember. Gorman and Horan had one
drink, staying about 3 or 4 minutes, and they then
left.   Both were in civilian clothes, there not
being sufficient uniforms to clothe all the men in
the Post. About 5 minutes later a crowd of Irregulars
entered the public-house, firing on both Lieut.
Jones and myself. I was wounded by a Thompson Gun
after firing the contents of my revolver at the
Irregulars. Lieut Jones was then taken away, leaving
me alone and the next I heard was that all three,
 Lieut Jones, Sergt. Gorman and Vol. Horan had been
 executed by the Irregulars. I did not see Gorman
and Horan again after they had left the Public House,
neither do I know whether they were on duty or not.

Sgd. John Croke, Pte.

On March 13, 1923, three Republican prisoners held in Wexford Jail were executed by firing squad. They were James Parle (28) of Clovervalley, Taghmon; Patrick Hogan (20) of William St., Wexford, and John Creane (18) Clonerane, Taghmon.

The three had been arrested on February 15, and charged with possession of arms at the residence of Major Lakin, Horetown. They had been sentenced to death.

James Parle, an officer in the I.R.A., was a farmer and cattle-dealer. He had served in the Volunteers during the War of Independence and was second in command of Bob Lambert's Flying Column in the Civil War. Patrick Hogan was a farrier and worked for his father, Henry Hogan. John Creane also had been a pre-Truce Volunteer and was a shop assistant. At the time he had a brother in the Free State Army and another in the Civic Guards.

Top: James Parle
Middle: John Creane
Bottom: Patrick Hogan

Authenticity would describe this photograph of men engaged in bitter guerilla warfare. There is a clear suggestion of men "on the run", men in action, stopping for a spell in the safe house. There are no tidy clothes, uniforms, collars and ties. Apart from two snap shot smiles there is tension. The safe house at Kyle, Crossabeg, was their commander's own, Bob Lambert in the right foreground. The girls at the scene are from left, May McDonald of the New House, Saunderscourt; Jo Culleton, Ballylboggan; and Margaret O'Connor, Tinahask. The men of the column standing are John Walsh from (possibly) Ballydicken, Danny Nolan and Arty O'Connor, later proprietor of the Star Restaurant, South Main Street, Wexford. Seated, George Quaid, Ballydicken; D. Nolan (number two) Jim Murphy and Michael Flusk, John Street, Wexford, later Mayor of Wexford, GAA administrator and referee. *(Robert Lambert Collection)*

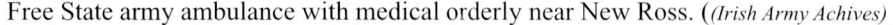

Free State army ambulance with medical orderly near New Ross. (*Irish Army Achives)*

McDonald's of Ferrycarrig (now the Oak Tavern) following the battle between the Free State Troops and the central Wexford Flying Column under Captain Bob Lambert.

Left: Dan Walsh, Kereight; Bob Lambert, Kyle; Laurence Walsh, Dublin. *(Robert Lambert Collection)*

Robert Lambert emigrated to Australia in the aftermath of the Civil War. Threats of turbulence presisted in the early thirties and the Fianna Fáil government created a new Irish Army Volunteer Corps. Robert Lambert was recalled to join the new unit with the rank of Captain. He was in charge of the Wexford Division.

(Robert Lambert Collection)

The leaf from a County Wexford War of Independence veteran's autograph book, compiled with many other famous names when prisoners of the British Army in the Curragh Camp, County Kildare, shows the signature of Harry Boland, Michael Collins, close companion. The date of Harry Boland's autograph is 24/8/1921. By the following August the horrifying change in circumstances are illustrated in what the

owner of the book added to Boland's signature. He has added the photograph with the following inscription. "Yet another martyr to Ireland's dreary long roll whose ghost will rise before us if ever again we attempt to sell our country. Rather than allow his country to be tricked into accepting the so called "Free State" he declared himself a Republican for which he was brutally murdered by his own countrymen!1/8/22. R.I.P. (Paddy Berry Collection)

Dan Walsh and Bob Lambert at the back of Walsh's of Kereight, Ballyhogue.

At Ferns in 1922. Captain Doyle (marked with X) later murdered at Enniscorthy while leaving evening devotions in the Cathedral and unarmed. *(Army caption)*

Locals and Free State soldiers push an artillery piece into position. This may not have been taken in County Wexford. The owner, Dr. "Pax" Sinnott, saw action in the South Tipperary Comeragh Mountains area which may account for it. It would appear to be a professionally taken photograph.
(Sinnott Collection)

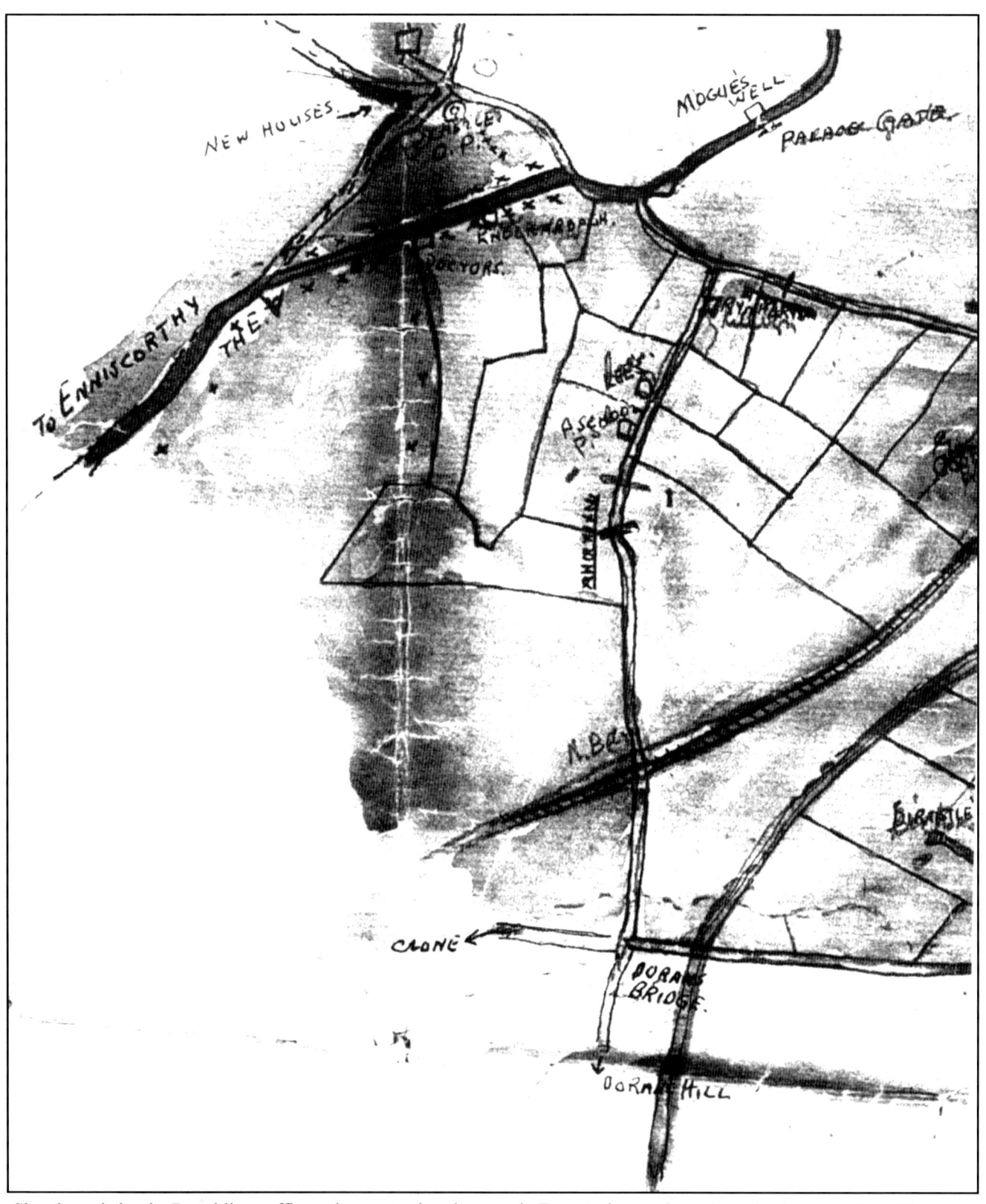

Sketch made by the Republican officers demonstrating the trees in Ferns to be cut down in ambush preparation. The imminent arrival of Free State troops was expected. *(Anonymous donor).*

The funeral of Commandant Peter Doyle, Free State army, of Ballinkill, Marshalstown who was shot in the grounds of St. Aidans's Cathedral, Enniscorthy, by republican soldiers on 10 October 1922. The burial took place in Marshalstown. The guard of honour officer in the foreground is Brigadier Joseph Cummins of Coolamain, Oylegate. Commandant Doyle's colleague, Captain Tom Doyle of Curragraigue, died from his wounds eight days after Commandant Doyle's death. The attack on the two officers' lives took place following the mission ceremonies conducted by the Vincentian Fathers. Five girls were injured during the exchanges, two of them seriously. *(Courtesy of Pat Codd).*

Free State soldiers drive through Ferns Co. Wexford August 1922.

Untitled, but presumably New Ross or Ferns. *(Courtesy Irish Army military archives, Cathal Brugha Barracks, Dublin)*

Comdt. Grogan and self May, 1923. (Co. Wexford. No further details) *(By courtesy Irish Army military archives, Cathal Brugha Barracks, Dublin)*

Engine trouble at Enniscorthy August 1922. *(Army caption)*

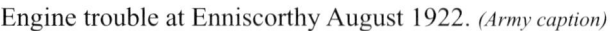

En route from New Ross to Dublin. Halt at Bray to mend a puncture. *(Army caption)*

The Free State Army enters Ferns August 1922 with Winchester repeaters ready for action.

Firing party at the graveside of Harry O'Connor accidentally shot at Crory, Ferns. He was interred in St. Mary's, Enniscorthy. Included are Thomas Roche, James Quigley, Michael Reddy, James Jordan, Matthew Flynn, Myles Moore, Patrick Maguire, Aidan Kirwan. *(Courtesy of Wexford County Museum)*

Relatives and a friend at the graveside of Volunteer Harry O'Connor.

Ballynastragh, the ancestral home of the Esmondes, was built in the 17th century and enlarged in 1767. It was burned along with its family documents, historical records and extensive library by anti-treaty forces on 9th March 1923. In the words quoted by local historian, Michael Fitzpatrick, "It is in the irony of things that this latest victim (Sir Thomas Esmonde) was himself one of, if not the only begetter of the Sinn Féin movement in its intellectual and educative beginnings, and indeed withdrew for a time from John Redmond's party of which he was a member for many years, on account of its want of understanding of the aspirations of Arthur Griffith and his friends."

On 28th January 1923 the Cliffe mansion, Bellvue House, Ballyhogue was torched by anti-treaty forces. Reduced to a roofless shell, the attackers nevertheless created a fire break between the residence and the beautiful Cliffe family oratory designed by Augustus Welby Pugin. It survives today as a chapel of ease and a favourite venue for weddings.
(Dan Walsh Collection)

June 1923, and Wexford's old jail is packed with republican prisoners. In the cell later occupied as a workers' canteen the white-washed wall had a pencilled calendar inscribed alongside the name P. Parle, Taghmon. The days of June 1923 were crossed but by the last week of June the inscriber was either freed, escaped or transferred. This little gem was white-washed over in the "improving" nineties.

Erskine Childers, the eminent English writer, provided Co. Wexford with arms following his gun running expedition to Howth and County Wicklow for the Irish Volunteers. *(Shane Sinnott Collection)*.

Jimmy Dillon, Harpoonstown, who was a lieutenant in B. Company, 3rd Battalion, South Wexford Brigade, IRA during the Civil War. He was the youngest prisoner in Maryborough Jail.

(Richard Roche Collection)

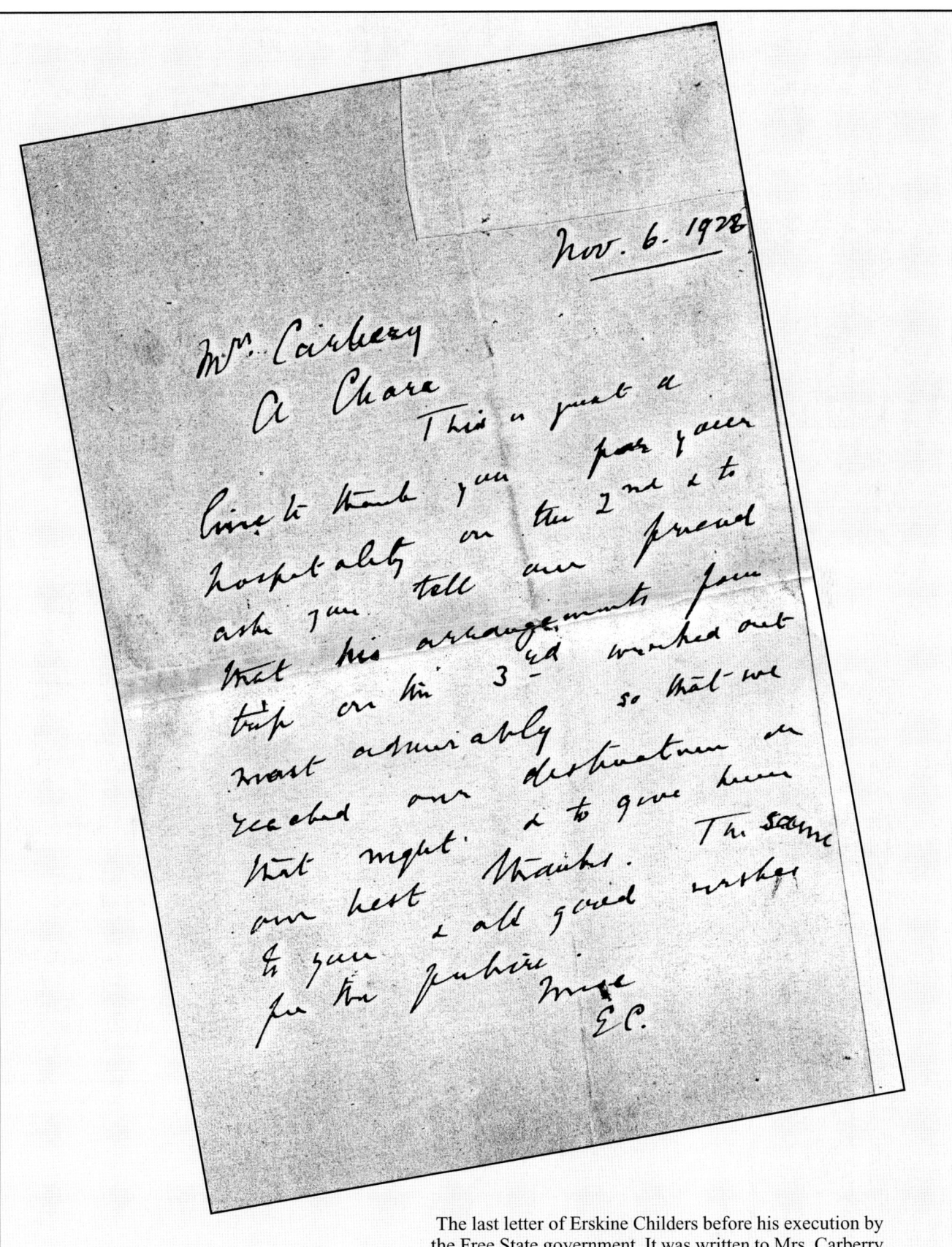

The last letter of Erskine Childers before his execution by
the Free State government. It was written to Mrs. Carberry
of Dunmain, Gusserane, Co. Wexford. *(Sinnott Collection)*

Liam Mellows delivering an oration at Wolfe Tones grave at Bodenstown in June 1922.

Mellows was elected a T.D. for East Galway and Meath in the 1918 election. On 2nd October 1920 he left America and sailed home, using a seaman's passport in the name of Edward Moore.

After his arrival home he was appointed director of purchases, charged with the responsibility of importing arms and equipment for the bitter struggle with the Black and Tans. He was also appointed to the Army Council. Liverpool was the centre of his activities and he regularly visited England and Scotland in pursuance of his work. Friendly seamen on many ships helped to get the arms to Ireland.

He was vehemently opposed to the signing of the Treaty, and his anti-treaty speech in the Dáil was one of the most powerful and impressive. On December 7th Sean Hales, T.D. and Patrick O'Malley, of the pro-treaty side, were shot in Dublin. Hales died. The next day, December 8th 1922, four prisoners, Liam Mellows, Rory O'Connor, Dick Barrett, and Joe McKelvey were taken out at dawn and shot as a reprisal.

CEASEFIRE, APRIL 1923

Wexford was devastated by the loss of its most active War of Independence veterans, many of whom had taken the anti-treaty side. Captain Bernie Radford and Lieutenant Con McCarthy were killed in action against the Free State soldiers at Spencerstown. The heaviest loss was that of Commandant Michael Radford, O.C, Third Battalion, South Wexford Brigade, IRA. He had taken part in the massive escape of Republican prisoners from Wexford Gaol on 2 May 1923, two days after the ceasefire of 30 April 1923. He was killed while taking evasive action from Free State soldiers on 22 June 1923 near Tacumshane. On the Free State side was his old comrade in arms, Captain Tom Cousins.

The Civil War had ended in 1923. Bitterness and disillusionment thrived on all sides as the dream of an independent 32-county republic evaporated. Political activity, however, commenced. Although refusing to take the oath of allegience to the Crown and remaining outside Dáil Éireann, the anti-Treaty TDs remained a large block of deputies. The photo from Gorey show Eamon de Valera with supporters. He had been released from prison by the Free State

Government on July 16, 1924. Included in the photograph taken in the grounds of Dr. E. G. Connolly's house are Dom Sweetman, OSB; Marie Comerford, Eamon de Valera, Dr. and Mrs Connolly, Mr. Roche, J. J. O'Kelly, Martin McGrath, Denis Allen, J. Fortune, Dr. James Ryan, Peter Connolly, Dr. O'Sullivan and Thomas Funge. *(Michael Fitzpatrick Collection)*

AFTERMATH

On the way to Courtown Harbour, or perhaps Castletown, in 1924. The photograph shows two future Presidents of the internationally recognised Republic of Ireland, one a President of the League of Nations, Eamon de Valera, with colleague Sean T. O'Kelly, then at the lowest ebb of their political careers. Pictured with them are Fr. Costello, A. Woods and Charles Murphy. They visited the grave of Seán Etchingham at Courtown, aferwards calling on Mrs. Etchingham, the deceased's mother. He also visited Mrs. Mellows, motherof Liam and Barney Mellows at Castletown. Mr. de Valera had just been released from prison. *(Michael Fitzpatrick Collection).*

1923. New Dimension. With the arrival of independence the Free State government logically introduced a new focus on the Irish language. All teachers trained under the old regime now had to have a proficiency in Irish. To accomplish this they were trained in groups, prudently divided into male and female. Our group has Miss Mary Victoria Sherwood, third from right at the back, later Principal in St. Iberius Chruch of Ireland National School, St. Patrick's Square, Wexford. She quickly became fluent, with the pleasing "blas" as well.

Normal service resumed. Shoppers returning from Wexford to the Fort of Rosslare on market day in 1924. In 1925 and 1926 the Fort village and its portion of Rosslare peninsula were swept away.

(Alice White Collection)

1924. The Ancient Order of Hibernians club premises were located in Mary Street, Wexford, at the old town wall (in background) where The People Newspapers offices are today. It was a social club for Catholics and Nationalists, many of whom were "Redmondites". They held many tennis tournaments, dances, social events and catered generally for the middle class. There were clubs all over County Wexford which catered for all classes, politics ranks and tastes, a study of which certainly deserves publication. The A.O.H., as it was called, declined and was gradually wound up in the 1930s.

The founding of the Army School of Music. Standing, left to right, Professor John Larchet; Commandant F. Sauerzweig and Denis McCullough of Belfast, President of the Irish Republican Brotherhood, married to Una (Agnes) Ryan of Tomcoole. Seated, Mary Josephine "Min" Mulcahy, nee Ryan, Tomcoole; Col. Fritz Brase; General Richard Mulcahy, Minister of Defence and Mrs. Larchet.

(Risteard Mulcahy Collection)

The Minister for Home affairs in the Free State Government, Kevin O'Higgins, addresses the first batch of unarmed Gardai to be commissioned in the Phoenix Park Depot, 1924. *(Sinnott Collection)*

Gardai in rural Wexford. Either Bridgetown or Kilmore Quay provide a first photograph of posted Gardai in 1924. Our donor, Brendan Barry of Pinewood Estate, informs us that the Garda seated on the right is his father Tom Barry. We cannot specifically identify the other three men. According to the Garda records for Wexford, number one district, all the Gardai were unmarried, a state of existence which did not survive for long.

Garda Síochána, Wexford, 1928. Photographed by Charles Vize, Wexford and Enniscorthy, in the Lower George Street Barracks yard, now Pembroke House, Abbey Street, Wexford. Back row, left to right: Gardai P. Cooney, D. Minogue, D. Sexton, P. Loughnane, D. Carey, J. Carey, F. McCarthy, T. Kennedy and J. Gribben. Middle row: Sgt. P. Heil, Gardai P. Wall, C. Geary, C. Driscoll, M. Kennedy, M. Boyle, J. Lafferty, P. Doolan and J. O'Brien. Front row: Gardai P. Nolan, P. Barry, Sgt. J. Kelly, Supt. J. J. Murphy, Inspector E. Lambert, Sgt. M. O'Brien, Sgt. P. Murphy and Garda J. McHugh.

A LIST OF GARDA STATIONS AND PERSONNEL IN CO. WEXFORD 1925

Chief Superintendent - Mr. Liam Stack, Wexford.
Enniscorthy District - Superintendent Kilroy, IC.
Enniscorthy - Sergeant Patrick Brogan, Gardai T. Rourke, P. Fingleton, B. McTiernan, J. Connolly, Edward Murphy, M. Whelan, P. Keogh, J. Minogue, J. O'Shea, P. Donnell, P. Wall, D. White.
Bunclody - Sergeant P. McDonagh, Gardai M. Power, E. Healy, E. Whelan, J. McCabe, M. O'Carroll.
Clonroche - Sergeant J. Quirke, Gardai B. Reynolds, M. Drew, J. Walsh, Richard McCarthy.
Blackwater - Sergeant D. Cahill, Gardai T. Roberts, J. Carey, T. Nolan, J. F. Kelleher.
Ferns - Sergeant P. Barrett, Gardai P. Frawky, J. Cully, P. Nolan, M. Hayes.
Killanne - Sergeant T. Howard, Gardai D. Daly, T. O'Reilly, J. O'Riordan, J. Carnew.
Oulart - Sergeant M. Mclnerney, Gardai J. Connolly, J. Walsh, T. McCarthy.
Oylegate - Sergeant James Dowd, Gardai J. McCarthy, M. O'Connor, M. Kelly.
Gorey District - Superintendent O'Neill, 1C.
Gorey - Sergeant T. Byrne, Gardai T. Kerrigan, J. Regan, M. Gibbons, J. Neylon, P. King, J. O'Brien.
Camolin - Sergeant Murphy, Gardai P. McSweeney, Edward Donelan, W. Kidney.
Clonevan - Sergeant J. O'Connor, Gardai T. McCarthy, M. Dwyer, P. Kelly.
Courtown Harbour - Sergeant W. Brophy, Gardai J. Donnelly, P. Kinsella, W. Purcell, T. O'Connor.
Coolgreany - Sergeant C. O'Sullivan, Gardai E. McGonigle, W. Laffan, T. Kelly, J. Daly.
Hollyfort - Sergeant D. Dempsey, Gardai J. Grimes, M. White, E. Malone.
Wexford District - Superintendent Downey, 1C.
Wexford No 1 - Sergeant J. Kelly, Sergeant J. Lyons, Sergeant E. McConnell, Sergeant C. Keogh, Gardai M. Boyle, M. Byrne, F. McCarthy, D. Sexton, T. Kennedy, G. Geary, C. O'Driscoll, P. Doolan, E. Riordan, J. Lafferty, J. O'Brien, Richard Downey, J. Dunjea, E. Kavanagh.
Wexford No 2 - Sergeant J. Barry, Gardai D. Byrne, E. Joyce, D. Carey, M. Spillane, D. Murphy, P. Deegan, P. O'Toole, D. Desmond.

Castlebridge - Sergeant M. Brennan, Gardai J. Behan, B. O'Connor, J. Godkin, P. Byrne.
Bridgetown - Sergeant J. Walsh, Gardai J. Histon, J. O'Leary, P. Smith, P. Barry.
Killinick - Sergeant Guinnane, Gardai J. Agar, T. Ward, P. Murphy, J. Hogan.
Kilmore Quay - Sergeant M. Bucktey, Gardai J. King, M. Moylan, P. Prenderville, M. Burke.
Duncormick - Sergeant J. Quinn, Garai J. Murray, A. Daly, P. Sheehan, T. Reale.
Rosslare Pier - Sergeant J. Dwyer, Gardai D. Minogue, P. Tuite, J. O'Connor, Richard Sinnott.
Taghmon - Sergeant W. Maher, Gardai M. Lynam, P. O'Brien, T. Tobin, M. Henehan.
Killurin - Sergeant T. Troy, Gardai P. Ahearne, T. Prior, J. Walsh.
New Ross District - Superintendent Kissane, 1C.
New Ross - Sergeant P. Hurley, Sergeant T. Byrne, Serge≤ant D. Somers, Gardai C. Harkin, P. J. O'Reilly, J. O'Mahony, T. Moylan, C. Cavanagh, M. Hunt, D. Daly, W. Prior, C. Driscoll, P. Nolan, D. Norton, J. McCourt.
Campile - Sergeant J. V. Hassett, Gardai P. Kenny, H. Rafferty, C. McCaffrey, D. Cronin.
Carrick-on-Bannow - Sergeant D. O'Donnell, Gardai J. Feeban, P. Barry, T. Madden.
Adamstown - Sergeant F. Mahon, Gardai M. Downing, J. McHugh, J. Neylon.
Ballywilliam - Sergeant T. Kelly, Gardai J. Lynch, D. O'Keeffe, M. Sheehan.
Ballycullane - Sergeant D. Ginty, Gardai J. McLoughlin, J. Mahony, T. Carroll.
Ballinaboola - Sergeant T. Dunleavy, Gardai E. Barry, T. Doyle, S. Bell.
Fethard - Sergeant M. O'Gorman, Gardai D. Dennehy, C. O'Sullivan, B. Sweeney.
Duncannon - Sergeant J. Littleton, Gardai W. Hennessy, E. Kennedy, C. McCarthy.

A CIVIL WAR LAMENT

The G.A.A. continues to be Ireland's most successful sporting body. It has had its share of criticism, much of it ill informed. One of its great and largely unheralded achievements was the bringing together of the opposing sides after the tragic Civil War. With brother pitted against brother, families, parishes and sporting clubs split and on conflicting sides, the G.A.A. played a prominent part in healing deep wounds and hastening the return to normality in the 1920's and '30's. *This song was commissioned by producer/director Tomás McAnna for the 1984 pageant 'Purple and Gold' (written by author, writer/broadcaster Nicky Furlong) and first performed in that production by the great Wexford ballad singer Paddy Berry.*

SLOWLY- with feeling. AIR - The Bantry Girl's Lament

LYRICS - Tom Williams

1.

The meadow grass has not been cut, the headland's overgrown,
The soft red apples lie despoiled on my mother's orchard ground,
And Autumn's sun, its short day done, casts shadows all around.

2.

The old folk tend the pastures now for the young men all have gone,
To fight in grief for their belief, to right the ancient wrong,
My brother, with his Thompson gun, faced me across the moor,
And against God's will, I shot to kill, my sorrow will endure.

3.

The crossroads where the dancing feet sent echoes down the lane
Are empty now and many a brow is racked with woe and pain.
Oh! who will cross the wide divide and take my brother's hand?
Oh! who was with him when he died, near the Slaney's shifting sand.

4.

How can we heal the broken rifts that separate us now?
For friend fought friend to a bitter end, can we smile again and how
Can hate and fear of yester-year diminish in our minds
The Civil War, what was it for? it broke the tie that binds.

5.

But the ash tree lives and its seedling gives a hope to boy and man,
And virgin spring a healing brings to the fields where the hurlers ran,
And meadow wide meets sharpened scythe and the fields are tilled again,
And carefree sounds from the sporting grounds come echoing down the lane.

Correspondence Vol. 3 (1996)

LUFTWAFFE CRASHES IN COUNTY WEXFORD.

Tel. (01)8324325

89 ABBEY PARK
BALDOYLE DUBLIN 13

28 December 1997.

Mr Nicholas Furlong
Drinagh Lodge
Wexford.

Dear Mr. Furlong,
You very kindly replied to my letter of 22nd September on the 2nd October. I had asked you would it be possible to obtain copies of some photographs published in *Wexford in the Rare Oul' Times*. You mentioned certain conditions which I consider to be more than generous. You mentioned that you would be in touch. I now realise that perhaps that you were awaiting my confirmation, which I am agreeable to. Your recent appearance on Mike Murphy's radio programme reminded me that I had not heard from you.

I studied the photograph of the remains of the Heinkel III on p34 and I am convinced that it is not the aircraft of the crew as stated in the caption. My research would indicate that this aircraft is Heinkel III werke nr. 3664 from 3/K.G.27 "Boelcke" which force landed on Rostoonstown Strand on 3 March 1941. It was flown by Lt. Freddie Heinzl and had been damaged during an attack on shipping off the Welsh coast, one crewman was killed during the attack namely Uffz. Gerd Rister. The other crewmen were Ofw. Rudolf Hengst, Ofw. Arthur Voigt and Gefr. Max Galler. The crew removed their dead comrade and then set fire to the aircraft. This is the same aircraft showing the fin and rudder as on p41 in which the werke nr. is clearly shown. I think that you will agree that the topography on p34 is quite different to that as seen for the Heinkel crash of 10 June 1941.

I find it all most interesting and hope to hear from you.

Yours sincerely,
A P Kearns

5 Loiscarrig Drive,
Cahersalee
Tralee,
Co. Kerry.
20/10/97

Dear Nicholas Furlong,
Following our telephone conversation on Saturday last I am enclosing some photocopies from yours and John Hayes' book in which I have written the correct information to go with the photos. On page 34 of your book you list the names of the Luftwaffe crew who died in the Carnesore crash, some of these names are misspelled. The crew were as follows; Uffz. Alois Mittermaier, Ogefr. Hubert Modrzejewski, Uffz. Josef Niebauer, Ofw. Ruddf Peschmann and Major Dr. Herbert Rumpf.

Dr. Herbert Rumpf was not a civil servant but a meteorologist, whose job it was to collect information for the Luftwaffe and Navy. Weather information was very important when planning U-Boat and air raids on Allied targets.

From the four German air crashes in Co. Wexford only one survivor is still alive and his name is Rudolf Hengst. After the war he married an Irish woman.

Yours sincerely,
Justin Horgan.

The precious snapshots of Luftwaffe funerals in Wexford, WW2, are part of the John Brendan Nolan bequest. The occasion is fully described in Vol. 3 County Wexford in the Rare Oul' Times (Furlong and Hayes 1996). The photos were snapped by John Scanlon.